I0037354

Forex Trading Crash Course

A Beginner's Guide to Learn All Forex Strategies, Trading Tools and Money Management. A Step by Step guide to Achieve the Financial Freedom

Roman Schmidt

© **Copyright 2019 - All rights reserved.**

The content contained within this book may not be reproduced, duplicated or transmitted without direct written permission from the author or the publisher.

Under no circumstances will any blame or legal responsibility be held against the publisher, or author, for any damages, reparation, or monetary loss due to the information contained within this book, either directly or indirectly.

Legal Notice:

This book is copyright protected. It is only for personal use. You cannot amend, distribute, sell, use, quote or paraphrase any part, or the content within this book, without the consent of the author or publisher.

Disclaimer Notice:

Please note the information contained within this document is for educational and entertainment purposes only. All effort has been executed to present accurate, up to date, reliable, complete information. No warranties of any kind are declared or implied. Readers acknowledge that the author is not engaged in the rendering of legal, financial, medical or professional advice.

The content within this book has been derived from various sources. Please consult a licensed professional before attempting any techniques outlined in this book.

By reading this document, the reader agrees that under no circumstances is the author responsible for any losses, direct or indirect, that are incurred as a result of the use of the information contained within this document, including, but not limited to, errors, omissions, or inaccuracies.

Table of Contents

Introduction

Is keeping your emotions in check the best way to trade in the Forex market? Do you really need a trading strategy to win big in currency exchanges? How should you read Forex charts? When you're a beginner in Forex trading, you may feel overwhelmed and lost in a sea of digital numbers.

Forex trading, or currency trading, is all about numbers, rates, trends, profits, and losses. The last one is an exception, though. You won't experience grave losses if you have an effective trading system in your arsenal. With enough funds, you can continue sailing in the sea. If you must lose against a wave, you must minimize your losses, and save your remaining funds in order to stay afloat.

Exchange rates are like the waves in an ocean. They go up, and they go down. Sometimes, they remain still. As a Forex trader, you have to take advantage of each big wave. Sell when the price is right and buy when the rate is low.

Many things can influence the height, strength, and speed of a wave. The same thing can be said with the rate of a currency pair. Politics, economic events, news, and even social media can affect exchange rates.

So, if you think that the value of USD will increase against the value of other major currencies tomorrow, think again because Forex trading doesn't work that easily.

Several factors can affect an exchange rate. These factors move prices upward or downward. Indicators, on the one hand, function like a map. They guide traders when charting trends. Ultimately, indicators can help you determine when the best time to take a short or long position is.

Forex trading can give you high returns, but it requires time, patience, and knowledge. If you're not equipped with the right tools, strategies, and know-how when trading currencies, your money will just go down the drain.

With the right trading strategy, coupled with a keen eye for spotting deviations and analyzing trends, you can win big in your Forex transaction. If you want to know more, then don't stop reading.

This book contains numerous guides and tips for currency trading. Thanks for downloading this book, I hope you enjoy it!

Chapter 1

<u>What Is Forex Trading?</u>

Forex (FX) trading, also known as currency trading, is a type of decentralized global market, wherein all the world's currencies are being traded.

The Forex market is probably the largest, most liquid market in the whole world. On average, its daily trading volume exceeds 5 trillion US dollars. If you combine all the stock markets around the world, they won't even come close to the sheer trading volume in the FX market. What does this mean to you?

If you have traveled abroad, you may have already made a forex transaction. For instance, you went to Paris, France, and you converted your US dollars into euros. Upon doing this, the exchange rate between the two currencies determines how much euros you will get for your dollars. The exchange rate is often based on the demand and supply in the market. Forex exchange rates fluctuate continuously.

Similar to stocks, the percentage of your shares to a corporation, you could trade currency based on your estimates. Being an equity investment, stocks represent part ownership in a corporation. This entitles you to a percentage of that company's assets and earnings.

However, there is one big difference between stock investing and forex trading.

With forex, you can trade up or down easily. The golden rules in FX trading are as follows:

-If you think a currency's value will increase, then it's good to buy it.

-If you think a particular currency will decrease in value, then you may sell it.

With the foreign exchange market being so large, finding buyers and sellers will be easy. Take the scenario below as an example.

In May 2020, Japan will devalue its currency to draw foreign businessmen and investors into the country. If you believe that this trend will continue for more than a month, then there are opportunities for easy Forex trading. In this case, you can trade by

selling the Japanese currency against the US dollar, Euro, or Australian dollar.

The more the Japanese Yen devalues against the currency of your choosing, the higher the profits you will earn. If Japan's currency increases in value while you're at an open position, then you will lose money. When this happens, it's best to opt for a close position.

What Is Forex Trading?

Day trading, stock dividends, stock investing—all of these are such a pain in the neck that you would wish you don't have to deal with them. This is why you should start with Forex trading instead. Mind you, this legit money-making scheme will not make you lose your shirt, car, or house if you do it properly.

Forex or FX is a portmanteau of exchange and foreign currency. Forex is the process/act of converting one currency into another for various reasons. Hence, you engage in Forex trading when you're converting some US dollars into the domestic currency of another country.

As stated by the Bank for International Settlements, an international bank, 5.1 trillion USD is the daily FX trading volume. The Forex market establishes foreign exchange rates for all of the currencies worldwide. The "exchange rate" is the rate at which a currency can be converted into another. Forex rates are regarded as the value of a domestic currency relative to another currency.

As an example, the interbank exchange rate of 100 Japanese yen to the US dollar means that ¥100 will be exchanged for each 1 USD. In the same way, 1 USD can be exchanged for each ¥100. Hence, it can be said that the price of a US dollar in Japanese yen is ¥100.

Equivalently, the price of a yen in relation to dollars is $1/100.

When needed, the government can change the rate.

Exchange rates, including interbank and FX exchange rates, are determined in the Forex market. The Forex market--where currency trading is continuous 24 hours a day during weekdays--is open to a range of sellers and buyers. In Forex trading, the spot exchange rate is the current rate. The forward exchange rate refers to a rate traded and quoted within the day. However, its payment and delivery are made at a later date or time.

For every currency, the market determines its exchange rate. This includes all aspects of exchanging, buying, and selling of currencies at determined or current prices. The major participants in the Forex market are the major financial centers and international banks around the world. Round the clock, except for weekends, such organizations and institutions serve as trading anchors between various sellers and buyers.

Currencies are always traded in pairs. A currency pair is a quote of the exchange rate for two different currencies being traded in the Forex market. When someone orders a currency pair, the base (the first listed currency) is purchased, whereas the second currency in a pair (quote) is sold.

In a currency pair, the value of the base is being quoted against the second. The currency that has been listed first is referred to as the base currency; the second one is called the quote currency. Take the USD/JPY pair.

The USD is the base currency, and the JPY is the quote currency.

The EUR/USD pair is the most liquid pair in the world to date. The USD/JPY is the second most prominent currency pair. The Forex market doesn't set the absolute value of the currency. Rather, it determines its relative value by setting the price of the base when paid with the quote. For example, 1 USD is worth x numbers of JPY, CHF, or CAD.

As stated earlier, the Forex market operates on several levels, and involves banking institutions. These institutions are corporations that serve as intermediaries of economic systems. Price signals guide such systems when it comes to making decisions regarding distribution and investment. Prices, signals, and exchange rates are based on the supply and demand in the market.

Wherever two or more parties or entities engage in an exchange, that place or virtual space can be considered as a market. In other words, a Market is generally one of the numerous types of systems, institutions, and procedures by which parties can exchange services, products, and shares. Most markets rely on sellers.

The Forex market relies on both the sellers, buyers, and financial institutions that serve as intermediaries.

In the FX market, investors and brokers can facilitate trade. Like other types of marketplace, there are rules and customs that traders must adhere to when trading currencies. These include platform registration, competitive pricing, and proper quoting.

On Devaluation, Floating Rates, Open Position, and Close Position

By now, you may have a general idea of what forex trading is. To make learning simpler for you, do take things a little bit further. Get to know some terms that are extremely relevant to the foreign exchange market.

• Devaluation

When a country deliberately adjusts the value of its currency in a downward trend, that country is devaluing its currency. Nations with a semi-fixed or fixed exchange rate like North Korea and China utilize devaluation as a monetary tool.

The purpose of such a monetary policy is to maintain the value of the domestic currency within a narrow band. This is because fixed exchange rates offer greater certainty for importers and exporters. It also helps governments to regulate inflation rate. In the 1970s, many industrialized nations began using this system.

From the 1940s to the 1970s, the Bretton Woods Agreement,

the first system utilized for the regulation of monetary values between different nations, set the exchange rates between participating countries to the US dollar (USD). At that time, the value of USD was fixed to gold prices.

Between the 1950s and 1960s, the US's postwar payments surplus balance became a deficit.

Because of this, the periodic rate adjustments that were permitted under the Bretton Woods Agreement proved to be insufficient. By 1973, Richard Nixon, the then president of the United States of America, removed his country from the gold standard. This move ushered in the floating rates era.

Floating interest rates move up or down along with the market or along with an index. An index is an indicator or measure of something. Floating interest rates can also vary, depending on the period/term of the debt obligation. This is in contrast with fixed interest rates, wherein the rate of the debt obligation remains constant throughout the loan's term.

Why do governments devalue their currency?

Unlike depreciation, a country will devalue its major medium of exchange to counter or solve a trade imbalance.

This happens when a nation's imports exceed its exports during a certain period.

Devaluation can reduce the cost of exports, making the country more competitive than other nations in the global market.

Then, the price of imported goods in that country will increase. Therefore, consumers will be less likely to purchase imported products.

In this case, domestic businesses will grow since imports decrease and exports increase. In conclusion, a nation that devalues its currency can reduce its deficit due to the increase in demand for cheap exports.

Depreciation, on the other hand, happens due to nongovernmental activities, such as the implementation of easy monetary policies.

In August 2019, the People's Bank of China (PBC) set the Chinese Yuan below seven per one US dollar for the first time in more than ten years. Due to this, global stock markets sold off. In the United States, the DJIA approximately lost 3% in 2019. The US called China a currency manipulator. Nevertheless, this wasn't the first time that China has devalued its fiat money.

Devaluation isn't all rainbows and unicorns, meaning that it has some negative aspects. When the prices for imports are increased, domestic industries become inefficient due to a lack of competition.

Higher exports can also bolster aggregate demand, inflation, and gross domestic product. Manufacturers may feel compelled to cut costs because exports have become cheaper than before. Due to this, the cost of services and products could increase as time passes by.

Hence, countries that have a semi-fixed exchange rate or fixed exchange rate utilize devaluation as a monetary policy tool. When a government devalues its domestic currency, the cost of that country's exports decreases and trade deficits shrink.

Devaluation can lower the value of a domestic currency against foreign currencies. Most significantly, the devalued currency will be

much lower than the country's major trading partners. With this, it's evident that devaluation can boost the economy of a country by decreasing the price of exporting. This enables domestic merchants to compete in the foreign exchange markets more easily than revaluation.

- Why Countries Devalue Their Currency?
- To shrink trade deficits and boost exports
- To decrease sovereign debt burdens
- To boost the economy

- Open position

An open position is an entered or established trade that has not yet become close to the opposing trade. Until an opposing deal occurs, the position stays open. This can exist after a sell (short position) or a buy (long position).

You can hold an open position for minutes to years. The duration will depend on your objective and trading style. However, the longer the position is held, the riskier the trade becomes.

- Close position

A close position is the opposite of an open position. When investors and traders transact in the Forex market, they're opening and closing positions. The first position that a trader takes is the open position. It stays open until someone buys all of the units he's offering. When an investor takes his deal and trades with him/her, the position becomes close. This implies that the trader has sold his/her financial instruments.

Transacting in the Forex Market

In the background, banks turn to financial firms and other small institutions that are known as dealers. They're involved in trading large quantities of Forex. Most dealers are medium-sized, local, or rural banks. These behind-the-scenes trading spaces are often referred to as the "interbank markets." In some cases, financial firms and insurance companies are also involved.

Trades between dealers can be large. The transactions sometimes involve hundreds of millions of US dollars.

Forex markets assist investments and trades. One of their core features is currency conversion. For instance, a brokerage platform allows an SMB located in the US to import products from EU member states. With FX markets, business owners residing in other countries can buy goods from Eurozone members in Euros even if their income is in USD.

In addition to that, the foreign exchange market also supports the carry trade speculation, as well as the direct evaluation and speculation of currency values.

As a trading strategy, a carry trade involves borrowing at a low- interest rate and investing in an asset with a high rate of return. It's based on borrowing in a currency with a low-interest rate, and then, converting the amount into a different currency. If the 2nd currency offers high interest, the proceeds (revenue) are placed on deposit. This could also happen if the proceeds are deployed into assets-- bonds, stocks, commodities, and real estate--that are denominated in the 2nd currency. In this case, everything will depend on the differential interest rate between the original and second currency.

In a typical Forex transaction, one party purchases an amount of a particular currency by paying with a specific amount of another currency.

Simply put, foreign exchange trading is just direct access trading (DAT) of two types of currencies.

What is direct access trading? DAT enables traders and investors to directly trade with another party, client, or market maker on the National Association of Securities Dealers Automated Quotations

System (NASDAQ). The NASDAQ was founded in 1971. It was the first-ever stock market in the world that uses an electronic system in providing stock quotes. Later on, it enabled investors to trade currencies and to execute buy and sell orders for over-the-counter stocks. Being a premier stock exchange, trading on this institution can give traders a feeling of assurance since it eliminates the need for brokers.

Components of a Forex Transaction

In the Forex market, currencies are always traded in pairs. The two currencies in a pair are inseparable; they're always together.

That is to say, you can't force to exchange your money with a currency that is not included in a pair.

For example, you want to buy a certain amount of Cuban peso using Malaysian ringgit. However, SMN/RM is non-existent.

Therefore, you can't trade your Cuban peso with the Malaysian ringgit.

The currencies in a pair are always traded against one another. The rate at which they are being bought or sold is referred to as the exchange rate. Currency supply and demand directly affect the exchange rate in Forex markets. Often, a Forex deal has three components and has three basic elements:

- Exchange rates in the FX market

Foreign exchange rates always change; they fluctuate every day. When you choose a pair, its exchange rate tells you how much of the second currency you need in order to obtain one unit of the base currency. You can't reverse the order of the currencies in any given pair.

Hence, you can just either sell it or buy it. Of course, this depends on the direction of the transaction. With the JPY/USD pair, you can only purchase JPY with USD. If you want to do the opposite, you have to choose the USD/JPY.

On trading platforms, such as XTB and CMC markets, you can view the available pairs for the currency you want to obtain.

For example, the exchange rate for EUR/USD is 1.5, implying that you need 1.5 USD in order to purchase 1 euro. If you sell 1 euro, you add 1.5 USD to your account.

Remember that all Forex deals involve buying a currency and selling another simultaneously.

If the value of EUR rises by 0.01, then the rate of exchange is now 1.26. For every 1 EUR you've bought, you earn 1 cent. If you trade oppositely, you lost 1 cent, for you've purchased euro for 1.56.

- What's a pip?

PIP stands for Point in Percentage. It is the most basic unit in the Forex market. In the foreign exchange market, currency pairs are often quoted to the 4th decimal place. A pip is the last and the smallest of the four numbers after the whole number. It's in the ten-thousandths place. For example, the exchange rate for a pair is 0.5678. The pip here is number 8. A pip is also referred to as "one basis point" or "1/100th of one percent."

Although a pip has a very small value, you can use pips for high leveraging. A difference of one pip can result in a significant loss of profit. This is especially true when you're investing a large sum for a particular currency.

Being a standardized unit, pips prevent huge losses. If a pip is equal to ten basis points (BIPS), a one-pip difference will make the exchange rate volatile. The higher the volatility of an exchange rate is, the riskier the transaction will be.

If the exchange rate for the USD/EUR pair is 0.8849, you can purchase 0.8849 EUR for 1 USD. If there is a two-pip increase in the exchange rate, the US dollar's value will rise relative to the euro's. Hence, you could buy more euros with 5 USD.

When trading large amounts, a one-pip or two-pip move can be significant to you. For example, you buy 15,000 euros with US dollars. Then, the amount you will pay is $13,273.50. If you purchase 15,000 euros again two days later and there is a two-pip increase, then you have to pay $13,276.50.

In such a case, the pip value is $3.00. If you purchase 200,000 euros at the initial rate and purchase the same amount again after a two- pip increase, then the pip value is $40. The pip value increases when the exchange rate for the base currency rises as well.

•   Points and Ticks

"Pip," "point," and "tick" are words you can use to describe price movements in the foreign exchange market. Although analysts and traders use the three terms similarly, they're different from one another.

Similar to a pip, a tick also represents a tiny measure of a price move in a quote/rate on the right side of a decimal point.

A point, on the one hand, is the smallest price move on the left side of a decimal point. It's the number in the ones place.

Of the three measurements, a point is the largest price movement. A pip and a tick only refer to changes to the fractional part of a quote. For example, the initial rate of a pair was 12. Three days later, it became 15. In this situation, you can say that there was a three-point movement, instead of a $3 movement.

Traders generally use the point to describe price changes in the foreign exchange market. With indexes, you can track price movements in points.

An index is like an indicator. It measures changes in a securities market. A Forex index evaluates and shows the performance of a particular currency against other currencies. It represents the percentage change in a currency's value against its major competitors.

The IG index or the investment-grade index tracks price changes to the fourth decimal. It represents pips, ticks, and points.

Top Transaction Types in Forex Trading

- Forward transaction

Forward transactions are deals made for the future. Money won't be involved in the transaction until a specified later date.

The seller and the buyer agree on a particular exchange rate for the agreed-upon date. The exchange rate can't be changed, so the market numbers on the trading day don't matter. The limits are defined by the seller and buyer.

- Spot transaction

Spot transactions or spot trades are the fastest and quickest methods to exchange currencies. In this type of Forex transaction, you purchase foreign currency for delivery on a particular spot date. The spot date is the day when the deal will be settled. It's also the day when the payment for the exchange will be transferred.

- Future transaction

As you would've thought, forward transactions are also future transactions. They're both considered as financial contracts. They are similar in nature. Such contract lasts until a specified time.

Future transactions are considered majors in the FX market. This means that Futures and Forwards often involve major currencies.

However, there are some differences. Future transactions are standardized, while forward contracts can be negotiated privately. In addition, forwards are bought and sold in over-the-counter markets.

Futures, on the contrary, are traded on regular Forex markets.

- Swap transactions

Swap trades are the most common Forex transactions. However, swap transactions can be risky since preliminary agreements are not carried out on an exchange or platform. Two traders agree to transact and exchange currencies at an agreed-upon date. On trading day, they will conduct the exchange.

- Options transaction

Like swap transactions, options are common in foreign exchanges. The Forex option gives traders the right to trade money on the market. This right or option has a specified date and a fixed exchange rate.

This type of transaction generates a lot of money and traffic on FX platforms and marketplaces daily.

Buying an option provides the right, but not the obligation to buy or sell the asset in question.

Forex options refer to the purchasing and selling of a right. After payment of the option fees, you can exchange a specific currency at the agreed-upon rate on a given date.

Understanding Micro-Lot and Other Small Units

Trading in micro-lots enables you to buy and sell in small units. What's a micro-lot? In a Forex trade, it is 1,000 units of the base currency. You can also trade in nano lots (100 units), standard lots (100,000 units), and mini lots (10,000 units).

Commonly, Forex is traded in lots. Lots represent the number of currency units you can buy or sell. Micro lots allow for smaller positions and greater fine-tuning of the trade than standard lots. When you place an order for a micro lot, you have ordered 1,000 units of the currency that is being sold or bought. For example, in the JPY/USD (Japanese yen versus the US dollar) pair, the JPY is the base and you either sell or buy 1,000 JPY.

A micro-lot is the smallest block of currency that you can trade. It's typically used by beginner and cautious traders who want to enter the market, but are trying to reduce future losses. Big-time investors also order in micro-lots when they don't want to trade standard or mini lots. Ten micro-lots are equal to 10,000 units or one mini-lot. Therefore, ten mini-lots is equal to one standard-lot.

You can manage risks when you trade in smaller units. For example, a two-pip move in the EUR/USD pair with 100,000 units may result in a 20 USD loss or profit. If you only have 500 USD in your account, a 10-pip move against the seller will make him/her lose twenty percent of their account.

Typically, mini-lots require 20:1 leverage. In this particular case, each pip move in the aforementioned currency pair results in a 1 USD loss or profit. The price needs to move fifty pips for the account to lose ten percent of its original balance.

The above examples show that micro-lots, being a small unit, can be beneficial to investors with a low-budget or a small account. Micro- lots reduce leverage and offer flexibility. They can also decrease the risk of a drawdown or losing a lot of money.

If your account has 500 USD, you only need 2:1 leverage to trade 1,000 units of a micro-lot. Purchasing a standard lot with your 500 USD account means that the leverage is 200:1. Hence, a 50 pip move can wipe your entire account. In the USA, as well as in many other countries, leverage in the foreign exchange is capped at 50:1.

In finance and economics, leveraging is the act of borrowing an amount in order to invest in something. In Forex trading, investment money is often borrowed from a financier, broker, or brokerage firm. Like in other global markets, high leverages are available in currency trading.

In contrast to small leverages, high leverages enable you to control and build up a large amount of profit. The major principle behind leveraging is quite similar to investing. The higher the amount of money invested, the higher the profits received.

More often than not, investing in micro-lots don't restrict traders. In fact, you can trade as small or as large as you want. You can trade 1 or 2 micro-lots or you can trade 1,000 micro-lots. With this flexibility, you can customize position sizes, such as 135 micro-lots. This is equivalent to 13.5 mini -lots.

If you can only trade mini-lots, instead of micro-lots, you need to choose either 13 or 14 mini-lots. This is not as exact as 135 micro- lots. Small brokerage accounts enable traders to buy or sell micro- lots with just a few hundred bucks, such as 100 USD or 500 USD.

In terms of position sizing, the size within a financial portfolio is the amount that you're willing to trade. Position sizing is integral to any investment type.

Position sizing is closely associated with Forex trading and day trading.

It's ideal to use micro-lots in position sizing so that you can efficiently fine-tune risks. For example, you want to purchase GBP/USD at 1.55 and set a stop-loss order at 1.50. The stop-loss you've placed will limit your losses. Placing an order for ten percent below the predetermined price will limit your loss to only ten percent.

A stop-loss order is a great tool for novice investors and those with a limited budget. Aside from this, you can also calculate the risk of a transaction using pips and position size. To know the best position size in a transaction, just use the formula below.

Dollars to risk\(micro-lot pip value X risk in pips) = position size in micro-lots

Here is an example equation:

40 USD/ (0.10 USD X 50 USD) = 8 micro-lots

In the example above, the trader is willing to risk 40 USD on the deal. For the above transaction, the position size is eight micro-lots. If the pip value of a move is $0.80 and you lose 50 pips on eight micro-lots, you'll lose $80. You can also use this formula to calculate the position size in a standard lot or a mini lot pip value. Remember that pip values may vary since they're based on the exchange rate of the pair that is being traded.

Defining Price Action

On a chart, price action is the movement of the exchange rate of a currency pair over time. Price action structures the technical analysis of a security. Short-term traders rely on trends and price action to device trading strategies and make decisions. As a practice, technical analysis is derived from price action.

Chart patterns and formations under technical analysis are based on price action.

Moving averages is a technical analysis tool for informed trading decisions. It involves the use of past prices in calculating and predicting future price movement and price action.

Investors utilize charts for plotting prices over time. With charting, they can interpret breakouts, reversals, and trends. The candlestick chart, for example, helps in visualizing price changes. It also displays close, high, low, and open values.

The engulfing pattern, Harami cross, and three white soldiers are candlestick patterns. They're examples of price actions that can be interpreted visually. You can also apply the same formations to other charts, such as box plots, box charts, and figure charts.

Technical analysts use data from a price action in order to calculate some types of indicators. For example, an ascending triangle, which has been applied to trend lines on a chart, can be utilized to foresee a breakout. Price action can indicate how many times bulls attempted a breakout.

Bulls are investors who think that a particular currency will rise. They invest in a security assuming that they can sell it at a high price in the future. When bulls engage in a breakout trade, they enter a long position after the price "breaks" above resistance.

Conversely, they enter a short position after the security breaks below the support level.

•   Resistance and support basics

The concept of resistance and support trading levels are integral in technical analysis. They are used in the analysis of chart patterns. You can also use them to determine price levels on barrier charts.

This prevents the exchange rate of a particular currency to be pushed to a specific direction.

Financial analysts use the said concepts to determine price points in a chart, in which odds favor a reversal or a pause of an existing trend. When a downtrend pauses because of an increase in demand, support occurs.

Resistance, on the one hand, transpires when the uptrend pauses for a brief period. This is largely due to supply concentration on the market. Both resistance and support areas are identified on charts with the use of moving averages (MAs) and trend lines.

The goal of technical analysis is to find order or trend in the random movement of price actions.

•   Using price action

Trend and swing traders work closely with price action. Unlike other traders, they often avoid fundamental analysis to focus solely on resistance and support levels in order to predict consolidation and breakouts.

In truth, the interpretation of price action depends on the trader. It's common for two traders to arrive at a different conclusion even after analyzing the same price action. One may see a near-term turnaround, while the other sees a bearish downtrend.

In addition, the time period used also influences the trader's perception since a security can have several day-long downtrends while maintaining a three-month old uptrend.

Nevertheless, always remember that foresight made using price action is speculative in nature. This means that swing traders invest based on conjecture, instead of knowledge. In this case, the investment made involves a high risk of loss. Speculative investors, or speculators, trade currencies in the hopes of profiting from future market value changes.

Economists estimate that approximately ninety percent of the daily trading volume in global Forex markets are based on speculations.

Chapter 2

How Did It Evolve Over the Years?

Forex Trading has been around for thousands of years. The oldest record of currency trading dates back to the Babylonian period (1895 BC – 539 BC).

Today, foreign exchange markets are the biggest and most accessible markets in the whole world. Over the last century, they've been shaped by major global economic events, namely the gold standard, the Bretton Woods Accord, the Great Depression, and many more.

History will repeat itself, as the saying goes. As a beginner Forex trader, you need to learn and study the key historic events that have molded the modern Forex market to what it is today.

Similar phenomena could occur in the future. Significant global events could greatly impact the landscape of currency trading.

Study the past so that you can formulate efficient trading strategies for the future. Dominate the foreign exchange market with your knowledge of past economic events.

Where Everything Began

According to renowned anthropologists, including Marcel Mauss and Bronislaw Malinowski, barter, a system where traders directly exchange services or goods for other favors or commodities without the use of money, is the oldest medium of exchange.

This practice began in the Neolithic period. Six thousand years ago, the descendants of the first farmers started to form complex communities.

Agriculture played an important role in everything that you have today.

You could attribute the conception of agriculture to the Natufians, and the barter system to the Mesopotamian tribes.

The first farmers were originally hunter-gatherers. Around 9,000 BC, they started to live sedentary lifestyles. After the conception of agriculture, several technological advancements were made.

Tilling the land led to the invention of complicated crude tools, such as the plow and the scythe. Agriculture also allowed people to have surplus products.

With excess food, the Natufians stopped traveling from place to place. Instead of caves and temporary lean-tos, they needed storage rooms, strong houses, and weapons for guarding their goods. Life became easier for them. Food became abundant.

With these, they started to settle down. In such conditions, there was no more need for infanticide since the adults could feed more mouths.

With the increase in human population and the demand for specific skills, such as blacksmithing, farming, livestock raising, etc., communities became complex and the barter system was developed.

Mauss proposed, in his 1925 essay titled "The Gift: Forms and Functions of Exchange in Archaic Societies that the practice of barter began around the 6th millennium BCE. Spices, salt, and Iron pyrite became prominent mediums of exchange during those days. Ships that carried sacks of the said commodities sailed to nearby fishing villages and city-states. According to Mauss, this could be one of the earliest forms of foreign exchange.

In the 6th century BC, the first-ever gold coins were made and produced. This coinage served as a form of currency. Unlike bulky goods, gold coins have certain characteristics.

The gold coins were acceptable, durable, divisible, uniform, and portable. Because of these characteristics, people from all walks of life accepted the coinage.

However, gold coins had one undesirable characteristic. When traders had to transport thousands of gold coins, chests would be required. When the coins were held in a small container, it became hard to transport them. And, they attracted looters and bandits.

Later on, the silver and copper coinage was introduced. In the 1800s, many countries, including the US and the UK, adopted the gold standard.

The Gold Standard

Being a monetary system, the gold standard guaranteed people that their government would redeem any amount of paper money. Under the gold standard, any domestic currency had a value that was linked directly to gold.

With this system, many nations around the world agreed to convert bank notes into a fixed amount of gold.

Any country that utilized the gold standard had set a fixed price for the precious metal. They then bought and sold gold at that fixed price, which was used to determine their currency's value.

For example, before the 1930s, the United States of America set the price of gold at 500 USD an ounce. Hence, during those times, the value of one US dollar would be 1/500th of an ounce of gold.

The system worked well until World War 1.

However, to pay for war reparations, many European countries, including Germany and Austria-Hungary, suspended the gold standard. They made this move in order to print lots of paper money for the repayment of their debt and to get richer.

But, there was one problem with this financial strategy. Printing more money than the standard rate caused inflation or hyperinflation.

Before World War 2, Germany experienced hyperinflation.

When a country prints more money, its economic output didn't increase. It only increased the number of banknotes and coins circulating in the economy.

When there was more money in an economy than what was allowed, consumers would be able to demand or purchase more goods than before.

However, in such a case, manufacturers responded by increasing the price of their products. Simply put, an increase in printed money can cause inflation. How can this happen?

For example, an economy produces 15 million USD worth of books. The price of each item is 15 USD. By this time, the amount of money circulating in the country is 15 million USD. If the government doubles the supply of paper money, the number of books won't change. In such a scenario, 1 million books will be sold at 30 USD.

Now, the economy is worth 30 million USD; however, the number of the product is still the same. If there is inflation—a general increase in prices of commodities and a fall in the purchasing value of money

—then the value of the country's currency will decrease. Take what happened to Germany as an example.

The inflation in Germany was almost at 100 percent, while in the UK, the inflation rate at that time was zero percent.

This implies that the price of German commodities doubled when compared to the prices of products made and grown in the UK.

Now, it's clear to you that printing money just makes goods more expensive than before. Hence, the increase in Gross Domestic Product is just an illusion.

GDP or Gross Domestic Product is the total market or monetary value of all finished services and goods within a country's border in a particular period. It functions like an economic snapshot and comprehensive scorecard of the economic health of a country.

As an inclusive measure of the total domestic production in any nation, GDP can be utilized to estimate the size and growth rate of an economy. It can also be adjusted for population and inflation estimates.

When the quantity of products does not change and the government prints more money than the standard number allowed, inflation can occur. If inflation is high, then it becomes difficult to make transactions.

Prices will go up frequently, and firms will often change their price lists as well. Before the 2nd World War, prices rose regularly in Germany.

And, workers got paid twice a day.

The prices of goods were so high that bills had to be loaded onto wheel-borrows when buying groceries.

In addition to that, the price of bread doubled within a week. This was very destabilizing for Germany's economy, and it created confusion and uncertainty.

If a country has high inflation rates, investors and entities will be discouraged to make investments.

That time, the inflation rate was so high in Germany that paper money was used as toilet papers. In the last quarter of 1923, the Germans had to carry cash in sacks and on wheelbarrows.

At times, people would be robbed of their bag, and the bundles of money were just left on the streets.

In 1922, Weinar Germany printed more money to meet allied reparations. This move by the government caused the hyperinflation in the early 1920s. This led to the collapse of Germany's economy.

Types of Money

Today, there's no country in the world that is using the gold standard. Great Britain stopped using it in 1931. The US followed the example of the UK in 1933. By 1973, they abandoned all of the remnants of the said monetary system.

The gold standard backed foreign exchanges only until 1971. In the same year, US President Richard Nixon closed the gold window. He took the world off the gold standard, which couldn't stay afloat during world wars.

The banknotes that were redeemable for a fixed weight of gold were considered valuables. This major economic event in the 1900s was known as "The Nixon Shock."

Many nations did not expect Nixon's bold move. It sent shockwaves and changes in the global economic system. When he took the gold standard, all of the currencies in the world had no backing in gold.

Hence, the exchange rate for every pair couldn't be calculated by simple arithmetic since their values depended on various factors. Governments controlled most of the factors. These factors are discussed in chapter 3.

• Fiat Currencies

At that point in time, countries around the world needed a system where exchange rates could be determined in real-time and were based on data flowing through global markets. The Forex market filled up this role.

The Forex market became integral to the world when Nixon took the gold standard from it.

When currencies were still backed up by gold, there were no foreign exchange rates. When the old monetary system was removed, only then that "pairs," wherein there is a base (nominator) and a quote (denominator), were introduced.

With fiat money, currencies around the world floated freely and they had to be valued against another.

Fiat money replaced the gold standard. What is this?

Fiat money is a phrase used to describe a currency under a government order—fiat—a formal proposition or authorization. Under the fiat, the currency should be accepted as payment.

For example, the US dollar is the fiat money of the United States of America. For Nigeria, it's the naira.

In other words, fiat money is any currency that is being issued by a government. No physical commodity backs fiat currencies. Rather, they are backed by the administration of the country that issued it.

The value of fiat currencies is derived from the existing relationships between demand and supply, as well as the economic stability of the country.

The majority of currencies today are fiat money. These include the JPY, USD, and EUR. This new type of currency allows central banks to influence the economy greatly since they have control over how many banknotes can be printed.

Fiat currency has value due to the fact that the government that issued it maintains/regulates that value or since two parties in exchange agree on a rate.

In the past, governments minted coins from valuable durable commodities, such as copper, silver, and gold.

Fiat money, on the one hand, is irredeemable and inconvertible. Since it's not linked to any physical reserve, such as silver or gold stockpiles, it's at risk of losing value or becoming worthless due to hyperinflation.

- Today's Currencies

Having no commodity backing is the most undesirable characteristic of fiat money.

In contrast, currencies backed by gold has intrinsic value. This means that its fundamental value is its true and inherent price and is independent from market values.

If investors and people from other countries lose confidence in a country's fiduciary money, it will not have any value anymore. If a currency is backed by a physical commodity, the value of the fiduciary money will depend on its total market demand. Gold, for example, is used to manufacture jewelry, decorations, devices, computers, and other electronics. Hence, gold has high value to this day.

The intrinsic value of fiat money is very low. Its value is measured based on the production costs of coins and banknotes. Its nominal value, by contrast, is fixed at its creation. The legal value of a banknote or coin is indicated on its contractual right.

A contractual right, or financial instrument, is any monetary contract between two or more parties or entities. It gives rise to a financial asset of one party and an equity instrument (financial liability) of another. It can also be in a form of proof of ownership of something, such as shares and bonds. These are fixed funding instruments that are representing a loan made by an investor to a borrower. The borrower is often a governmental or corporate entity.

When it comes to fiat money, the country and its central bank guarantee its value. If financial agents stop trusting a nation or its major financial institutions, the currency will not have any value.

In economics, an agent is a decision-maker in an economic model. By finding the solution to an ill- or well-defined optimization (choice problem), agents can make decisions. Simply put, economic agents are merchants, capital markets, producers, influencers, and consumers.

The face value of currencies neither changes over time nor is affected by the owner.

Still, the purchasing power—the financial ability to buy products and services linked to the ownership of coins and banknotes--changes as time passes by.

To reiterate, inflation affects the value of a currency. The higher the rate of inflation is, the lower the purchasing power of holding coins and notes become.

Furthermore, any currency can depreciate on financial markets, such as the stock, bond, and real estate markets. Capital markets, including primary and secondary exchanges, are also considered financial markets.

When that happens, a currency loses its face value against another. Investors and agents compare the purchasing power of two currencies by using parity.

Coins and banknotes are used as payments in physical trades. Print paper and coins enable agents to trade goods or services. In this case, the value of the domestic currency is fixed within the country that issued the money. At the time of the issue, this is considered as the currency's face value.

- Legal Tender

This term is often confused with fiat money. However, they're different from each other, and these terms must not be used interchangeably.

Fiat currency is money issued by the administration of a country. With a government decree, it can be made legal tender.

A Legal tender, in the most essential respects, is any number of banknotes or coins that should be accepted if offered as payment of debts.

Law courts are required to recognize paper money and coinage that are treated as legal tenders as satisfactory payment for anything owed.

Essentially, legal tender is anything that is offered as payment for the extinguishment of a debt.

Contracts, tax payments, and legal fines are some examples of legal tenders.

In any country, the national currency is considered a legal tender. A statute establishes legal tenders. The statute specifies the thing or asset that is going to be utilized as payment.

It also determines organization or entity authorized to issue or produce it to the public. An example of such institutions is the US treasury and the Royal Canadian Mint.

Legal tender can also be used for currency manipulation and the issuance of monetary policies.

In the United States, the most-recognized legal tender always contains Federal Reserve coins and banknotes.

A court of law requires creditors to accept legal tenders to release personal debtors from liability, thereby preventing the creditor from making any more collection. In other words, a legal tender frees debtors from financial obligations and protects them from unlawful collection actions.

Nevertheless, private entities can refuse to accept legal tender if any state law does not prohibit their actions. This is possible when the customer has not transacted with the creditor yet and no debt has been incurred.

By design and by default, laws governing the issuance of legal tenders prevent the universal adoption of any asset, aside from the circulating banknotes and coinage in the economy.

Therefore, credit swipes and checks are not considered legal tenders. They only serve as money substitutes. They represent a medium whereby the check holder can receive legal tender in the future.

Also, cryptocurrencies, such as Bitcoin and Litecoin, are not generally accepted in most capital markets since they can't serve as legal tenders. In 2013, Jan Brewer, a governor in Arizona in the same year, rejected a bill that would've made silver and gold coins as legal tender in the said state, as an addition to the US currency.

USD is both legal tender and fiat money; it is accepted as payment for public and private debts.

Legal tender is any currency-issued-by- a-government that has been declared "legal." Many nations, including Switzerland, France, and the United Kingdom, issued fiat currency, and then made it legal tender.

They set their national currency as the standard for repaying debt.

In conclusion, you can only use the term "legal tender" as a substitute to the phrase "fiat money" when the government of the country in question declares their fiat currency as the standard for debt repayment.

Types of Money Used in Currency Trading

As a medium of exchange and a unit of account, three of the major types of money can be used in currency trading.

•   Commodity money

This is the oldest and simplest form of money. This type is backed by scarce or rare natural resources that serve as an intermediary instrument or store of value.

Commodity money originates from the barter system, and is often exchanged for goods and services.

In fact, commodities facilitate systems of barter or any type of transaction similar to it. To this day, barter is a generally accepted medium of exchange. It's still commonly practiced in 3rd world countries.

However, the intrinsic value of the product being exchanged determines its value. By this, the product or raw material functions as money. Shells, spices, gold coins, and beads are some examples of commodity money.

•   Fiat money

As discussed earlier, the value of fiat money is determined by a statute.

When a government declares a currency as a legal tender of the country, all citizens, organizations, and firms are required to accept it as payment. If they don't, they will be fined or jailed.

Unlike the first type, fiat currencies are not backed by a physical commodity. Also, they have a low intrinsic value.

The relationship between demand and supply determines its worth. This is the reason why the major currencies in the world like EUR, USD, and CAD have a higher value than others.

- Fiduciary money

To some degree, fiduciary money is similar to fiat money. You can call a fiat currency as fiduciary money, but you can't do the same to the latter.

Basically, fiduciary money could be a banknote or coin that is circulating in an economy or within a particular geographical area.

But, unlike fiat currencies, fiduciary money cannot be considered as a legal tender. This means that the government that issued the currency did not decree it to be a form of payment for debts owed.

Also, the law doesn't require citizens to accept fiduciary money as a remittance.

Still, the fiduciary issuer assures that it can be exchanged for a certain amount of fiat currency or commodity.

Drafts, banknotes, and cheques are examples of fiduciary money.

- Commercial bank money

Commercial bank can be utilized to purchase services or goods since it represents a portion of a currency made of debt, which commercial banks generate.

More specifically, fractional reserve banking, a process wherein banks provide loans, create commercial bank money.

In essence, it is debt that is generated by a commercial bank. You can use it to buy real money or exchange for goods and services. Book money is an example of this type.

Key Events in History That Have Shaped the Forex Market

• Biblical Times

According to Archaeologists, currency exchange and trading first transpired in ancient Babylonia. The then money-changers--the merchants who helped people to exchange money--lived in the Holy Land. This was during Biblical times (the time of Talmudic writings).

Modern archaeologists call those people "kollybistes." They use city stalls for trading. During feast times, they utilized the Temple's Court of Gentiles.

More recently, it was discovered that goldsmiths and silversmiths also served as money-changers.

In the 4th century AD, the Byzantine government monopolized the exchange of currencies in Constantinople.

The artifact PapyrinPVZ I 59021 depicts the occurrences of currency exchange in Ancient Egypt.

Exchange and currency were integral to trading in the ancient world. Both enabled people to trade necessities, household articles, and luxury items.

Food, pottery, fabric, livestock, and raw materials are the most common commodities in the times of the Talmudic writings.

During those times, if a Greek gold coin was heavier than an Egyptian coin, then the trader could purchase more material goods using the Greek coin than the Egyptian coin. This means that the former had more value than the latter.

Based on that old system, world leaders decided to back currencies with gold.

•   Medieval Times and Later Years

In the 1500s, the Medici clan opened banks in foreign countries so that they could trade currencies. Their first and major bank was named "Medici Bank."

To manage foreign exchanges, Medici Bank launched an account book called "the Nostro." Nostro is the Italian word for "ours."

They also opened banks in foreign locations to trade currencies, acting on behalf of textile merchants. The account book contained two columned entries. These show amounts of local and foreign currencies and data about the recording and saving of an account with a foreign bank.

In the 17th and 18th centuries, Amsterdam, Netherlands maintained and regulated an active foreign exchange market. By 1704, currency trading took place between economic agents that acted on behalf of Holland and the Kingdom of England.

- Early Modern

Brown & Sons engaged in foreign exchange in 1850. At that time, they were the leading agents for currency trading in the United States.

Around 1880, Banco Espirito Santo, which was owned and established by J.M. do Espirito Santo de Silva, was permitted to launch a currency trading business.

Many economists and historians consider the year 1880 as the beginning of modern foreign exchange.

Aside from de Silva's Forex business, the gold standard was also implemented that year.

Before World War I, international trade had many restrictions. Most countries around the world have only a handful of legal trade relations.

- Modern to post-modern

From the late 1890s to the early 1910s, holdings—property, stocks, and other financial assets—of currency markets increased yearly at the rate of 10.8%. The value of gold also increased annually at a rate of 6.3%.

By the end of 1913, almost 50% of the world's Forex trades was conducted with the use of the pound sterling.

The total number of foreign-operated banks in London increased, from three in 1860 to seventy-one to 1913. Even so, London only had two Forex brokers in 1902.

At the beginning of the 1900s, thousands of people engaged in Forex in Berlin, Paris, and New York City.

Britain, on the other hand, remained uninvolved until 1914.

In 1922, the total number of Forex brokers in Great Britain increased to seventeen. By 1924, forty companies registered as Forex businesses.

The Kleinwort family, during the early 1920s, were considered as the leaders of the foreign exchange market, while the Seligman and Japheth, Montagu & Co. were still building their reputation and customer base.

When the number of firms that dealt with foreign exchange grew, trade in Great Britain started to resemble its modern status.

However, continental exchange controls and other factors in Europe and South America impeded attempts at prosperity from currency trading.

- Post World War II

Almost after the 2nd World War, in the year 1944, the Bretton Woods Accord allowed currencies to fluctuate within ±1% from their par exchange rate.

The United Nations Monetary and Financial Conference or the Bretton Woods Conference was the assembly of

730 representatives from forty-four allied nations. The conference was held at the Washington Hotel.

The hotel was located in Bretton Woods, United States. The major purpose of the conference was to regulate the financial and monetary order after the outcome of the World War.

Held from July 1 to 22 in that same year, the representatives signed accords that underscored the establishment of the International Monetary Fund (IMF) and the International Bank for Reconstruction and Development (IBRD).

The accord, as well as the system of monetary management, established a set of rules for financial and commercial relations among Japan, Australia, Canada, the United States, and Western European countries.

The Breton Woods Agreement of 1944 was the first-ever comprehensive negotiated monetary order. Its major purpose was to govern the monetary relations among independent nations.

The accord obligated all member countries to adopt or establish a monetary policy that could maintain foreign exchange rates within

±1%. This was possible by tying their domestic currency to the gold standard. The capability of the IMF to bridge the temporary balance of international payments (BOPs) also helped in implementing the policies.

In addition, the Bretton Woods Agreement also addressed the non- cooperation of other countries.

As a whole, the accord prepared the world for the economic impact of World War II and established sets of procedures, rules, and regulations for the world's largest economies, including Brazil, France, India, Germany, Japan, China, the UK, and the US.

It helped stabilize the economy of many nations.

For this to happen, the agreement and the system of monetary management paved the way for the establishment of the IMF and the World Bank.

Back in Japan, the Forex Bank Law was introduced nine years after World War II ended. Because of this, the Bank of Tokyo, a Japanese foreign exchange bank that operated from 1946 to 1996, became the nation's center of Forex transactions.

Four years after its establishment, Japanese law allowed currency trading with many Western currencies. The country opened its borders for international trade.

In 1971, Richard Nixon ended the Bretton Woods Accord and the fixed rates of exchange. This resulted in the creation of free-floating currencies.

In 1971, the Smithsonian Agreement allowed for the fluctuation of rates by up to ±2%.

From 1961 to 1962, the US Federal Reserve's volume of foreign operations was still low. The financial organizations involved in managing and controlling exchange rates concluded that the restrictions of the said agreement were unrealistic.

Hence, the Smithsonian Agreement ceased operation at the end of the first quarter of 1973.

Sometime afterward, not even one of the major currencies of the world, including USD, EUR, and CAD, had the capacity for gold conversion. Many countries and financial institutions depended on currency reserves.

From 1970 to 1973, the foreign exchange market's trading volume increased by three-fold. According to Gandolfo, a w-tier currency market was created and subsequently introduced with dual currency rates. However, like the Smithsonian Agreement, this was abolished as well.

In June 1973, Reuters, an international news agency in London that was founded in 1951, introduced computer monitors. This replaced telex and telephones used for quote trading.

- After 1973

In 1st world countries, state control of Forex trading ended by 1973. This event was largely due to the free and floating market conditions of the modern era.

According to some sources (cite this), the first-ever currency pair trade was conducted in 1982. By 1983, other currency pairs became available.

On the 1st day of January 1981, the People's Bank of China allowed domestic enterprises to participate in Forex trading.

At some point in 1981, the government of South Korea stopped controlling Forex trades. They permitted free trade in the country for the first time ever.

In 1988, South Korea accepted the International Monetary Fund quota for international trade.

In 1985, some European banks, including the Bundesbank, intervened and influenced the Forex market.

In 1987, the greatest volume of all Forex trades occurred in the United Kingdom. The United States followed and was ranked second in terms of having the greatest proportion of currency exchanges.

From oil trade to foreign exchange, Iran modified its international agreements with some countries in 1991.

Financial Bubbles

A financial bubble is a period of price increases and rapid expansions, which are often followed by a market contraction or slowdown.

Bubbles, as well as manias, have existed since the boom of the very first financial market.

Severe market crashes are mainly due to human nature. Overselling, hyperinflation, and terrorist attacks can affect the stability of a market.

Throughout human history, the Bitcoin and the Tulip are two of the most unusual bubbles in terms of price appreciation and asset type. Both are considered unusual assets.

Bitcoin is the most successful decentralized cryptocurrency to date. On the other hand, the tulip mania was very unusual in the sense that fashionable tulip bulbs were regarded as highly-priced commodities.

The first-ever recorded speculative bubble, the Tulip bulbs mania, dated back to 1636 – 1637.

Roughly 400 years later, the Bitcoin bubble deflated. It reached its crest in December 2017. From 0.003 USD, its price jumped to 19,000 USD in the last month of December.

Since then, the value of this cryptocurrency has kept fluctuating.

Among other historical bubbles, only Bitcoin's peak value rivaled and exceeded that of the Tulip bubble.

At the crest of the tulip mania, one tulip bulb could be sold for 10 times more than the yearly income of a skilled worker in the Netherlands.

In a few months after the craze started, the majority of the speculators—the people who invested in property, stocks, or other ventures in the hope of making a profit— couldn't afford the cheapest tulip bulbs. The market collapsed in February 1657.

The tulip mania and the Bitcoin craze are perfect examples of how the nature of humans can affect marketplaces.

This conjecture stays true despite all the technological advancements and the availability of information and education to speculators.

The type of asset and reason behind the inflation of the financial bubbles are different. However, the general behavior of the participants in both markets is quite identical.

The same event could occur again in the near future

when another new asset or commodity is introduced to the world.

The Wall Street Crash of 1929

The Wall Street Crash of 1929 is the most famous stock market crash in history, and was the first one for the industrialized world.

The bubble burst on October 24, 1929. This date was later called the "Black Thursday." It also marked the onset of the Great Depression.

The 1929 Wall Street Crash affected the American economy greatly. In a few months after the crash, it destabilized many economies.

On Black Thursday, the stock prices in America started to go down. By October 29, the industrial average of the Dow stocks dropped by roughly twenty-four percent.

Affecting the confidence of investors in Wall Street markets, the Crash triggered the Great Depression.

The principal trading dates were Black Thursday, Black Monday, and Black Tuesday. The last two were the worst days for the Dow in history.

The overconfidence of investors in the stock market during the first few years of the 1920s created the unsustainable financial bubble that burst on the night of October 24, 1929.

Within 24 hours, many lost their investments, life savings, and businesses.

On that same date, the Dow Jones, a stock market index, like the Russell 3000 and the S&P 500, fell by eleven percent. This signaled a stock market correction.

In finance, a ten percent decline in the value of a security from its most recent crest is called "stock market correction."

A correction occurs when there is a need to reserve individual assets. A market, index, or asset can fall into a correction for months, weeks, or days. On average, market corrections are short- lived and usually last between two to four months.

Analysts, investors, and traders utilized charting methods in order to track and predict corrections. Many economic factors can cause a market correction. From wide-scale macro-economic shifts to errors in a corporation's management plan, the cause behind a market correction is varied.

The crash in 1929 was largely due to the unsustainable boom of stock prices in the previous years. The irrational demand of investors and their over-confidence in America's economic growth cause the boom. The market participants in the Wall Street market crash bought stocks on the margin.

As reported by CNBC in 2018, the S&P 500's average correction only lasted for four months.

The value of stocks fell by thirteen percent before recovery. Nevertheless, it's a piece of cake to understand why a novice investor would worry about a ten percent decrease in the value of portfolio assets.

In contrast, seasoned investors don't worry much about a two-month or a three-month correction. However, there are instances when a correction serves as a precursor to a global recession.

On Black Thursday, the Dow Jones opened at roughly 300. Immediately, stock prices fell by eleven percent.

As a result, bankers bought stocks to improve the prices. Trading tripled in volume. The strategy did work, but on Black Monday, the value of the stocks went down again. This time, it decreased by roughly thirteen percent.

On October 23, 1929, The Washington Post headlined "Selling Waves Creates Panic due to the Collapse of Stocks." By October 24, one of the worst stock market crashes was recorded in history.

When the investors lost faith America's economy, foreign exchange rates were affected.

The crash was followed by a financial bubble. Since 1922, prices in the stock market had gone up by twenty percent annually until 1929.

In the roaring 20s, it was almost as if everyone invested. This was largely due to the financial invention referred to as "buying on margin."

"Buying on margin" is the act of borrowing money from a specific broker to purchase stocks. This is similar to taking a loan from a brokerage firm.

Margin trading enables traders to buy a specific amount of stock. The loaned amount is usually more than the borrower's net worth.

This enabled low- and middle-income individuals to invest in stocks. This way of investing resulted in the irrational stock buying in the roaring twenties. When panic selling reached its peak, the stock market crashed.

The main reason for the Crash was the speculative bubble that the credit stock purchase system fueled. The crash collapsed many of the world's economies, including the American, British, and Weimar economies.

In the next three years, the recession, which started in the US, spread like a pandemic worldwide.

At the start of World War II, which was largely caused by the stock market crash, the arms race boosted the major financial markets and economies in the world.

The Relationship between Stock Markets and Foreign Exchanges

In the last 100 years, stocks and currencies have been two of the

most traded securities in financial markets. It's evident that the rise and fall of stock prices affect the economies in the world.

To some degree, the volume of securities and the market sentiment in the stock market are also related to Foreign exchange rates. Trends in the stock market can be used to predict future price movements.

As stated, when domestic share prices increase, investors gain confidence in the economy of the given country. Foreign investors will take interest in investing in a country, and then, demand for the domestic currency will improve.

Conversely, when stocks underperform, the confidence of foreign investors falter. They reconvert their funds back to USD or other major currencies.

At times, the performance of a capital stock affects the value of a pair. For example, the Nikkei securities exchange in Japan has exhibited an inverse correlation with the USD/JPY.

This implies that a rise in the value of the Nikkei stock strengthens the Japanese yen against the US dollar.

Every time that a rally in the Nikkei stock happens, investors see the power of the JPY over the USD. As a result, they will withdraw their money from the USD and invest on the JPY.

When the value of the yen increases, the aforementioned currency pair weakens. This can be attributed to the decrease in the exchange rate of the base.

For some traders, the Nikkei index can be an indicator of the price movement of the USD/JPY currency pair. It is common for traders to buy USD/JPY when Japanese stocks are plummeting. Conversely, they sell USD/JPY when the Japanese stock exchange is beginning to strengthen.

However, the usual connection of stocks to the exchange rate of a particular currency pair changed during the onset of the 2008 Global Recession. When this recession affected the major financial markets of the world, the Nikkei stocks and the USD/JPY became linked positively, not inversely.

The stock exchange moved in the same line as the pair for the first time ever.

This rare trend is due to the change in attitude of most of the investors. They started to regard the Japanese yen more positively than before.

When trading, you need to look at the trends and the nature and behavior of the majority of traders after a major economic event. This implies that you have to consider various indicators before trading in the Forex market.

Based on the portfolio balance approach, any change in a nation's economy can impact the domestic currency and the supply and demand for foreign bonds. This shift in the price determination for bonds will then affect the exchange rate between foreign and domestic money.

The major advantage of this approach when compared with conventional analysis is due to the fact that financial securities tend to adjust faster to trends than to the availability of tradable goods.

Another example of the relationship between stocks and shares is the correlation between the British pound sterling and the FTSE 100 stock index.

This stock index is directly affected by the fluctuation of the value of the national currency. This is largely due to the fact that the majority of the 100 companies listed on the London Stock Exchange operate internationally.

Therefore, a large percentage of their profits are denominated in the US dollar and other major currencies.

If the pound sterling decreases in value, then the price of the FTSE 100 stocks will improve.

Still, don't forget that the foreign exchange market is volatile. Even if a major economic event impacts the stock market, the direct influence of the stock exchange will lag.

Until a particular international company or organization releases its financial report, investors won't be able to fully understand the degree of the effect of the stock market on the Forex market.

The stock market really does influence foreign exchanges. When you're using the trends in the stock market as an indicator for determining future forex rates, you must be cautious.

Other than the rise and fall of specific stock indexes, the stand of the United Kingdom in the Brexit and the EM economies can also be used for determination.

When the United Kingdom hinted that it would leave the European Union, the value of the pound sterling fell immediately.

When the domestic currency strengthens, the value of the stocks of the British companies with international operations drops.

Conversely, if the purchasing power of the British pound declines, then the profits of big UK companies increase. When their revenues increase, the value of their stocks rises as well.

GlaxoSmithKline is one example. The company generates most of its profits overseas.

For instance, the price of a GlaxoSmithKline (GSK) was roughly

£1400 one week before the actual vote. When the UK left the EU, the value of the British pound dropped. After this, the price of a GSK stock was £1709.

Despite that, the share prices of other companies decreased due to inflation. The fall of the British pound led to an increase in the price of domestic goods in the UK.

The inflation affected consumers the most. They had to spend less than usual. Hence, the revenues of some companies fell. In December 2017, the GSK share price returned to £1380.

There is also a connection between emerging markets and the value of USD. To this day, the US dollar is integral to the finances in emerging markets (EMs).

This is due to the fact that the USD is the world's reserve currency. The status of EM stocks is tied closely to the wealth of the USD.

The EM economy represents the wealth and resources of a developing nation that is becoming more and more engaged with international trade and global markets.

When capital flows out of the emerging markets, the exchange rate of the USD improves. Emerging markets rely on commodity exports. These are denominated in US dollars. When capital flight occurs, domestic stocks weaken and the USD rises.

In economics, capital flight is a wide-ranging withdrawal of capital and financial assets from a country. This happens due to unfair capital controls, currency devaluation, and economic or political instability.

Capital flight is only considered legal when foreign investors send their money back to their country. It becomes illegal when a government with unfair capital controls restricts the transference of assets out of the country.

Capital flight is a heavy burden to 2nd and 3rd world countries. Since it interferes with economic growth, it lowers the living standards of the citizens in the country in question.

Ironically, an open economy is the least vulnerable to legal or illegal capital flight. This is because openness and transparency attract investors. Often, investors become long-term prospects for domestic markets.

So far, there is no definitive and proven relationship between the Forex and the stock market. Over the years, some obvious correlations and trends piqued the interest of investors. However, the said correlations change at times, especially during a market crash.

It can be risky to rely on just one data marker. The relationships that exist between stocks and forex are prone to change.

As a trader, you have to consider multiple indicators, not just one, when trading. The trends in the stock market can be used as indicators when making a trading decision. You should look at other factors, such as moving averages, on-balance volume (OBV), relative strength index (RSI), etc.

The Great Depression

The Wall Street Crash of 1929 led to an extensive and long economic crisis—The Great Depression. This global phenomenon mostly affected developed nations, including the United States, Canada, and Weimar Germany, beginning in the early- to mid-30s. The recession in the USA spread across the world.

Just as the share prices of stocks fell, the value of the German mark declined. The great recession caused inflation in Germany. When the Weimar government devaluated their currency to pay loan interests and war reparations, the inflation turned to hyperinflation.

- America and Germany

As companies downsized or filed for bankruptcy, millions of Germans were left unemployed. Other people lost thousands, if not millions, as banks shutdown.

The horrible conditions led voters to look for a more radical alternative than democracy. Adolf Hitler and his Nazi Party became charismatic to the eyes of the desperate Germans.

The economic instability in Germany before World War II forced many companies to cease trading. Those who had stayed afloat somehow fired workers. Mass unemployment and starvation were the most visible effect of the Great Depression.

In 1932, over 11 million Americans were unemployed, and a piece of bread in Germany cost 1.20 USD. Today, that costs 15 USD.

Because of the dire situation in Germany, many people lost their confidence in banks. Vigilant ones rushed to withdraw their money right after the Crash. The unfortunate many lost their pensions and savings.

Germany's economy relied greatly on foreign loans. When the American economy collapsed, US financiers called in foreign loans. Germany's economic situation was not resilient enough to repay debts and interests.

In the roaring 20s, German industrialists enjoyed a time of prosperity due to foreign investments and loans.

However, in the 1930s, foreign investors called back their money. While credit and capital were nearly impossible to acquire, the demand for German products also waned.

To make things worse, the USA—the major purchaser of Germany's industrial exports—set high tariff barriers in order to protect US companies.

Consequently, German industrialists and manufacturers lost revenues from export sales. In 1933, twenty-six percent of the country's workforce had no job.

Similar to America, unemployment in Germany affected its citizens greatly. Food supply was enough, but not everyone can afford a loaf of bread or a slice of bacon.

Parents and orphanages abandoned children on the streets. Thousands of these street urchins died from malnutrition and disease. Millions of skilled workers spent years in idleness. White- collar jobs were also insufficient for all the professionals and fresh graduates in Germany.

The Weimar Republic did not respond efficiently to the Great Depression. Heinrich Bruning, the chancellor of

Germany from 1930 to 1932, feared budget deficits and hyperinflation more than unemployment.

Instead of creating jobs and stimulating the economy, the chancellor increased taxes to decrease budget deficits. He then implemented spending reductions and wage cuts.

The Reichstag, the parliament, rejected Bruning's policies. However, President Hindenburg supported the chancellor and issued emergency decrees.

As expected, Bruning failed the economy and the citizens of Germany. It failed to improve the country's budget. It just increased unemployment rates instead. The existing Reichstag parties bickered with one another and contributed to the instability of the country.

The real beneficiary of Bruning's disastrous policies was Hitler. The hard reality of the early 1930s had opened the eyes of millions of Germans.

Almost one year after the stock market crash of 1929, the Nazi party was able to dominate the Reichstag votation. They secured 230 seats.

• The gold standard and the spread of the global depression

The gold standard served as the medium for the global spread of the Great Depression. The Federal Reserve and some members of the international gold bloc set a deflationary policy. They allowed prices to fall by 1/3.

Modern economists believe that the said policy caused depression in Europe and the United States.

Plus, countries with healthy economies were forced to concede to the policies.

In the price-specie flow mechanism, nations that lost specific amounts of gold, but desire to maintain the gold standard, must allow their money reserves and the prices of their domestic goods to decrease.

Under the classic gold standard, a counterbalance flow of gold coins can offset the prices in a country. The flow of specie equalizes domestic price levels across numerous nations. This balances international payments and foreign exchange rates.

Gold was an efficient medium of trade on the national and individual levels. The exchange rate of currencies in the Forex market was based on their weight in gold.

For example, one French franc was equivalent to an ounce of gold. At the same time, one British pound equaled 1.2 ounces of gold.

That time, the exchange rate of the francs against the British pound could be calculated mathematically. The currency's name served as an assurance that the parties or governments involved would give the predetermined or agreed-upon amount.

This monetary system was efficient in many ways. It prevented market imbalances to grow.

If a country involved in a Forex transaction was importing goods or products from another, then the importer would have paid a large amount of gold to the exporter. This situation would deflate the domestic prices.

Likewise, there would be inflation in the exporting country due to the inflow of gold. Such a situation would increase the prices of commodities and make exporting expensive.

The gold standard prohibits unhealthy trade imbalances between two or three countries.

Aside from the price specie flow mechanism, the Smoot-Hawley Tariff Act (the US Tariff Act of 1930) and other protectionist policies further worsened the global depression.

The gold standard was rigid, however. This means that it suspended gold convertibility or devalued currencies in the terms of the monetary system.

During the crisis, all major currencies left the gold standard. The United Kingdom was the first nation to abandon the gold standard. They depleted their gold reserves due to speculative attacks.

- Speculative attacks

In the Forex market, a speculative attack is a sudden and massive selling of a currency. Foreign and domestic investors can carry out this attack.

A central bank or government ties the domestic currency's official exchange rate to the gold price in another country. This keeps the value of the currency within a narrow range.

In the 1930s, speculators targeted regimes with fixed exchange rates. This is due to the fact that their currencies were fragile. Their government can keep its currency and economy stable when there is no speculative attack. For example, Hong Kong pegged its HK dollar to the US dollar. The exchange rate was HKS 7.8 to USD 1.0.

The currency being targeted had an unrealistic exchange rate. In other words, its value was not sustainable. In case of a deflation or speculative attack, its value when compared to the major currencies would be in a pitiful state.

Before World War II, many central banks bought back their currency by paying with holdings of currency reserves. Holdings are contents of a financial portfolio. Portfolio holdings encompass various investment products, from stocks and bonds to options and ETFs.

If domestic or foreign investors think that the country's central bank doesn't have enough foreign currency reserves, they will target the domestic currency. In this case, the nation in question won't be able to defend its fixed exchange rate.

Speculators would sell the domestic currency (at a fixed price) in exchange for the reserve currency. They do this to deplete the foreign reserves of the country in question.

If its central bank runs out of currency reserves, it will be forced to let the currency float.

This, in turn, leads to depreciation—a decrease in the value of a currency relative to the currencies of other countries.

Developed nations have huge amounts of reserve assets, which are often called war chests. This is why speculators often target small nations since they could deplete their central banks more easily than 1st world countries.

When the UK faced speculative attacks in 1931, the Bank of England discontinued exchanging banknotes for gold. Later, it let the British pound float on Forex markets.

Japan and Scandinavia followed suit in that same year. Italy and the United States remained using the gold standard until 1933.

The countries under the "gold bloc" such as Belgium, France, Poland, and Switzerland stayed until 1935 or 1936. The major economies that left the gold standard earlier than others recovered quickly.

China, which relied on the silver standard, nearly avoided a depression.

- Breakdown of international trade

Economists stated that the downturn in international trade after the Wall Street Crash worsened the depression. This was especially true for countries that relied heavily on exporting such as Germany.

The nations that remained on the gold standard kept a fixed exchange rate and restricted foreign trading.

These countries did this to keep their reserve assets intact and stop economic decline. They restricted foreign trade. They also utilized protectionist policies to mitigate gold losses and bolster their balance of payments.

On the contrary, the countries that left the gold standard permitted currency depreciation. This strengthened their balance of payments and ratified new monetary policies. With the new policies, central banks could lend money to domestic companies at lower interest rates. By doing these, the countries were able to mitigate the effects of the crisis.

The depth and length of an economy's downturn and timing of its recovery are associated with how long it stayed on the gold standard. The countries that abandoned the system shortly after the Stock Market Crash of 1929 experienced early recoveries and mild recessions. Contrastingly, those that remained longer than others endured prolonged slumps.

- Effects of tariffs

According to economists, the Smoot-Hawley Tariff—The Tariff Act of 1930—aggravated the Great Depression. As mentioned in the website of the US Senate, this law is the most catastrophic tariff throughout the history of the American Congress.

The act increased US tariffs on more than 20,000 imported commodities and goods.

The tariff promoted American-made goods by increasing the prices of products from foreign goods. This protected US farmers and raised revenue for the federal government, but it failed to improve the living status of the majority of Americans in the 1930s.

The Bretton Woods Agreement

Based on the economic events in the inter-war years, US planners developed an economic security concept. This concept was developed to promote and enhance postwar peace. Cordell Hull, the longest-serving Secretary of State, was one of those who considered trade relations as something that could encourage world peace.

The Tennessee politician believed that trade warfare and economic discrimination had been the cause of World War I and II. This is largely true for World War II since Adolf Hitler, one of the two perpetrators of World War II, resented the Allied powers because of Germany's economic instability.

Hull argued that specific free trade agreements provoked the French, American, and German protectionist policies.

According to Hull, unhampered trade is linked with peace. On the other hand, unfair economic protocols, trade barriers, and high tariffs are agents of war.

He said, "if the flow of trade is free in the sense of fewer obstructions and discriminations so that no nation will be jealous of another, the standard of living of people worldwide may rise. Economic dissatisfaction, which breeds war, can be eliminated and long-lasting peace could be achieved."

Getting ready to rebuild the global economic system while the 2nd World War was still raging, 730 representatives from forty-four countries around the world gathered at Bretton Woods, New Hampshire, United States.

The conference began in July 1, 1944, and it ended in July 22, 1944.

The delegates signed the agreement on the 22nd day of July of that year. It was underscored in the agreement that the gold standard would be the basis for the USD. The other currencies, on the other hand, would be pegged against the value of the US dollar.

Establishing a system of institutions, procedures, and rules to manage the international monetary system, the accords established the IMF and the International Bank for Reconstruction and Development (IBRD).

Being an IFI, an International Financial Institution, the IBRD proffers loans to 2nd and 3rd world countries,

which are considered middle- income developing countries. This institution has been a member of the World Bank Group.

Like the other members—the IDA, IFC, ICSID, and MIGA—IBRD's mission is to eradicate poverty, support worldwide economic development, and bolster open trading between countries. This includes currency exchange.

Trade propels growth, reduces poverty, creates jobs, and increases the number of economic opportunities. More than 1 billion people have improved their status of living due to open trade since 1971.

The World Bank Group promotes international, open, predictable, and rules-based international trading systems. The organization aims to make global markets accessible to anyone in the world

Open trade, which is also sometimes referred to as speculative trade, is any transaction that hasn't yet been closed. For example, when you buy a stock and you want to resell it, you can consider the transaction as an open trade. The transaction remains "open" until the stock is actually sold, and the deal is ultimately closed or completed.

In finance, speculation is the act of conducting any risky financial transaction, which has a high probability of losing value. Despite this, open trade has also a high probability of gaining a major value.

Developing nations, including Afghanistan, Argentina, and Niger, struggle with intervening factors. Inflation, monopolies, and poor internet connectivity are some factors that prevent them from accessing foreign exchanges.

They impede people in remote areas from accessing Forex markets. Even a nation with transparent and liberal trade policies can suffer if its markets aren't interconnected.

Many impoverished people live in remote or landlocked areas. Such places have no international trade links or have poor internet connectivity.

One of the goals of the World Bank Group is to make foreign trading more accessible for everyone.

• The system explained

In 1944, the USA controlled 2/3 of the world's gold. They insisted that the system should rest on both the USD and the gold standard.

Soviet representatives, however, declined to accept the final accords. They charged that the financial institutions they had established were Wall Street branches. The world banks started to operate in 1945 after enough number of nations ratified the accord.

When Nixon announced that the United States of America would not exchange gold for USD anymore, the Bretton Woods System ended.

One of the primary goals of the delegates who attended the conference in 1944 was to establish an effective foreign exchange system. They hoped that the system would prevent competitive currency devaluation and promote global economic growth. These goals were of the greatest importance to the Bretton Woods Accord.

Two of the main objectives of the International Monetary Fund was to monitor currency exchange rates, as well as to recognize countries that desperately needed global monetary support. The World Bank, formerly known as IBRD, was established for managing funds for assisting nations ravaged by World War II.

At the start of the 21st century, the IMF had 189 members. Today, it's still supporting global monetary cooperation.

Together, the IMF and the World Bank promote fair trade and poverty eradication through their grants and loans to governments.

Although both the system and the accords dissolved in the 1970s, the IMF and the World Bank have become strong pillars for foreign exchange markets worldwide.

Regarding the pegging system, it's similar to other pegging regimes, wherein pegs of currency provide stabilization for goods, services, and money trades.

As stated earlier, all of the nations that had sent delegates to the conference agreed to a set rate versus the USD in which only one percent of diversion is allowed.

In conclusion, the Bretton Woods System reduced the volatility of foreign exchange rates. The system also improved international trade relations between countries. The stability of Forex markets was also a contributing factor for the capability of the World Bank to provide loans and grants.

Chapter 3

How Is Forex Trading Beneficial to the Financial Market?

More than a hundred years ago, institutional traders and large banks were the only entities that had the means to access Forex markets. Today, the recent technological advancements and the wide use of IoT devices have enabled small traders to take advantage of the various benefits of the foreign exchange market. Similar to NASDAQ, online trading platforms allow small traders to buy and sell currencies on the market.

Forex and the World

Most of the currencies of the world are on a flexible exchange rate. This means that the value of a currency of a particular country fluctuates in response to the latest trends and events that are related to the foreign exchange market.

A floating currency is the exact opposite e of a fixed currency. The value of the latter depends on material goods, another currency, or a currency basket—a portfolio of selected currencies with different weightings. Commonly, governments used the currency basket to reduce the risk of currency fluctuation

In the modern world, the most widely used currencies are floating.

These include the Swiss franc, the Indian rupee, the euro, the pound sterling, the Japanese yen, the Australian dollar, and the US dollar. Still. Even with floating currencies, central banks often participate in the foreign exchange market to influence the value of fluctuating exchange rates.

Worldwide, most nations have central banks. About seventy-five percent of the central bank assets are controlled by China, Japan, the US, and the countries in the Eurozone. A central bank is a national bank. It provides banking and financial services for its country's government and banking system. It also implements the government's monetary policy and currency issuance.

The Canadian dollar closely resembles an untainted floating currency. The central bank of Canada hasn't interfered with its value since 1998. The USD runs second to the CAD since the US made little change to its FX reserves. Forex reserves are assets and cash held by a central bank or similar monetary authority. The primary purposes of such organizations are to balance payments of the country, to maintain confidence in financial markets, and to influence the Forex rate of its currency.

Contrastingly, Japan and the United Kingdom intervene a lot. Japan is known for its systematic currency devaluation, and more recently, North Korea also devalued their won to curb inflation rates.

One of the largest and most influential macro-economic themes that affected automation suppliers was the devaluation of Japan's currency.

Both Japan and China are manufacturing economies. As stated earlier, exports become cheaper when the currency of a country is devalued. This increases the number of local jobs since tourists and that country's citizens use the local currency pay for local products. This improves the economy, curbs inflation, and increases demand. When demand is high, more job opportunities are available for the people.

In 1973, the Smithsonian Agreement collapsed, and most of the currencies around the world followed suit. Yet, some countries, like the Gulf States, fixed their currency to another currency's value. This, however, is associated with a slower growth rate. With a floating currency, targets, except for the exchange rate, are utilized to implement monetary policy.

Today, it's considered that the currencies all over the world are on a floating rate of exchange. They're always traded in pairs, such as Dollar/Yen, Euro/Dollar, etc. Approximately eighty-five percent of worldwide daily transactions involve Forex trading of major currencies.

Four currency pairs are often utilized for investment purposes. They are the following: US dollar against Japanese yen, Euro against the US, US dollar against the Swiss franc, and British pound against the US dollar.

In the trading market, they look like the following: USD/JPY, GBP/USD, USD/CHF, and EUR/USD.

If one currency will appreciate against another, it's recommended to exchange the quote currency for the base currency. By doing so, you can stay in it. In general terms, appreciation is the increase in an asset's value over time. In a floating rate exchange system, the changes in the value are based on demand and supply in the FX market. Appreciation is linked directly to demand. If the value goes up (appreciates), the demand for the currency rises as well.

If your predictions are right, you can initiate the opposite deal. This is done to exchange the first currency for the other and then collecting the profits from it.

Dealers at forex brokerage companies perform transactions on the FX market. Forex is integral to the world market. Hence, while you sleep in your bed, the dealers in the Eurozone are trading currencies with their American counterparts.

Clients can place stop-loss and take-profit orders with brokers. Brokers perform overnight executions. Price movements on the foreign exchange market are smooth. Unlike in the stock market, they don't have gaps every morning. New investors can exit and enter positions without encountering issues because the daily turnover on the Forex market is approximately USD 1.2 trillion.

In truth, the FX market never ceases to stop. The foreign exchange market is the oldest and largest financial market worldwide.

When you compare the Forex market with others, you'll see that the market for currency futures only comprises one percent of all Forex transactions.

Unlike the stock and futures market, currency trading is decentralized. This means that it isn't centered on any exchange.

Currency trading moves from major financial centers of the United States to Europe, Australia, and New Zealand, to Europe, and back to the US. It's a sort of a cycling trading game. In the past, the Forex inter-bank market was only available to large organizations. This is because of strict financial requirements and large minimum transaction sizes.

To reiterate, large financial institutions and major currency dealers were the only ones to take advantage of the Forex market's liquidity and the amazing trending nature of the world's primary currency pairs. However, today, Forex brokers can break down larger-sized inter-bank units. Because of this, they can offer total beginners and small traders opportunities to trade in small increments.

Brokers and trading platforms offer small-to-medium companies and individual spectators options for trading at the same rates and price movements. Two decades ago, only big players like banks dominated the Forex market.

The Role of the IMF and the World Bank in Currency Trading

The Bretton Woods Accord created two institutions that stood-the-

test-of-time. Since 1945, both organizations have served as integral foundations for international trade activities, foreign exchange, and capital financing.

In the 1930s, the Great Depression, which started in 1929 and lasted until the late 1930s, caused many economies to fail. It caused famine, high unemployment rates, homelessness, high tariffs, and World War II.

Since it's the deepest and most extensive depression in the 1900s, it's commonly utilized as an example of how certain events can cause an intense decline in the global economy.

Starting in the USA, after stock prices plummeted, the effect of the Great Depression was later felt in other countries as well. The stock market crash became global news in October 1929.

When a stock market crash occurs, a dramatic decline in stock prices will surely follow. This can happen across principal cross- sections of a stock market.

In turn, inflation will manifest and paper wealth will decrease.

Panic drives crashes, the same as underlying economic factors like wages, laws, policies, unemployment, governmental activity, and tax rates. These often follow economic bubbles—speculative bubble or mania.

A speculative mania is any situation wherein prices of assets are based on inconsistent or implausible foresight. A transaction in an asset or currency at a price range exceeding the intrinsic value of the asset or base can also be considered as an economic bubble.

When external economic factors are combined with mob psychology, in which selling by some traders drive fellow participants to sell as well, a long-term or short-term stock market crash can occur. This is often influenced by the following conditions:

-        A bull market, where stock prices continue to rise over a long period

-        Excess economic optimism, where price-to-earnings ratio (P/E ratio) surpasses long-term averages

The long-term average is the average price of a financial instrument, such as loans and bonds, over several months or weeks.

For example, you can compute the 200-day moving average (MA) by adding the closing prices from each day of the past 28 weeks.

Once you have the sum, divide it by the number of trading days.

Likewise, you can use fifty-, twenty-, or 100-day moving averages to calculate short-term and medium-term trends.

Forex traders use MAs to create simple trading strategies so that they can benefit from trading opportunities. A trading strategy is any method used for buying and selling in foreign exchange markets. One is often based on predefined rules utilized to create decisions.

Moving averages are primarily utilized as indicators for trends. And also, they are used for trading level support and resistance. These two are the most important elements in technical analysis—the analysis of chart patterns. All of these will be further discussed later.

The exponential moving average (EMA) and the simple moving average (SMA) are the most common MAs. The SMA is the average price over some time, while the EMA adds weight to recent prices. Both MAs serve as the foundation for several Forex trading strategies.

Although there are proven trading strategies during stock market crashes, such as selling calls and hedging with put options, the fall of domestic equity markets leads to a decrease in the inflow of funds from foreign investors.

As a result, the value of the domestic currency plummets.

This relationship between stocks and Forex markets can't be applied most times since stock markets around the world move in one direction. However, the inverse correlation between Nikkei stocks and the USD/JPY pair is one notable exception.

Wars, large corporate hacks, natural disasters, overselling, and federal laws and regulations can all affect the value of a currency.

It can either make or break the economy of a nation.

For example, the Wall Street crash of 1929 triggered a global Great Depression. The widespread poverty in Germany caused by the collapse and the inability of the USA to provide more loans to German industrialists strengthened the Nazi party. The effect of the Great Depression in Weimar Germany propelled Hitler to power.

Hitler's alliance with fascist Italy and his invasion of Poland sparked World War II. Nevertheless, America profited greatly in World War II.

The war raised the US economy from the brink of collapse. During the war, over 17 million civilian jobs were created. This increased the US's industrial productivity by ninety-six percent.

In addition to that, corporate profits also doubled. In fact, World War II and their arms trade helped in ending the Great Depression in the United States.

The US federal government became an influential economic actor that could regulate economic activity. Through spending and consumption, they partially controlled many economies of the world. The last World War revitalized many American industries.

By 1945, many sectors were oriented sharply to defense products such as electronics and aerospace. The effects of the war hampered the major economies of the world, except for the United States.

The majority of US industrialists and civilians enjoyed unprecedented political and economic power after 1945. This is also the reason why they exerted much influence in the delegation of the Bretton Woods Agreement.

The fall of the gold standard forced countries to devalue their currencies, reduce the usage of foreign exchange, raise trade barriers, and compete against each other.

All of these are contributing factors to the decline of world trade and the onset of the Great Depression. As stated, the Bretton Woods Accord established two institutions that became intergovernmental pillars that supported the world's financial and economic order to this day.

Both the IMF and the World Bank have expanding roles. Over the years, nations have requested to expand the responsibilities of the two organizations.

Today, the major economies of the world are still seeking for a single monetary agreement that is quite similar to the Bretton Woods system.

When the IMF interfered in Kenya, the Central bank there removed their control over capital flows—the movement of money for trade, investment, or business production. However, corrupt politicians took advantage of the situation. This was known as the Goldman scandal.

Proponents of free markets claim that capital markets should operate without intervention. According to them, efforts at influencing exchange rates worsen things; currencies should be allowed to attain their market level.

The IMF faced difficulties from 2008 to 2011 because of the global economic crisis. For the first few years of the 21st century, finance, foreign exchange, and global trade propelled global expansion and industrialization. This enabled many nations to repay their debts to the IMF. Many countries also utilized trade surpluses to amass FX reserves.

Forex reserves are cash and reserve assets held by a monetary authority, like a central bank. Foreign currencies, cash, and gold are some examples. They are readily transferrable and can be used for the following:

-        To influence the foreign exchange rate of a

currency

-    To balance payments

-    To maintain the trust of other countries in their financial markets

The USD, for example, is an anchor currency. This implies that banks worldwide hold it as a reserve currency. It can be used to influence monetary policies and back liabilities.

Many economists suggest holding FX reserves in a foreign currency. It's best to hold assets in a fiat currency not connected to the domestic currency.

Such assets are held to ensure that the government has backup funds in case of devaluation. It's common for central banks to amass reserve assets in their foreign exchange. These reserves are often held in USD because it's the most traded currency worldwide. FX reserves may also be denominated in the Euro, British pound, Chinese yuan, and Japanese yen.

Reserving foreign currencies can act as a barrier in case of a market shock.

As of May 2020, China has the largest FX reserve. Their reserve assets are worth more than $3 trillion. Much of their currency reserves are held in USD.

Japan follows China in terms of the amount of foreign currency being held as reserve assets.

If you combine the reserves of China and Singapore, the total would be $3.87 trillion. In truth, Asian nations dominate Forex reserves.

There are six Asian countries in Investopedia's top ten countries with the biggest Forex reserves. China, Japan, and Russia are in the top five. For these countries, it's easy to conduct international trade since most foreign trades and currency exchange involves the USD.

Being in the top five of the list, Saudi Arabia also holds a considerable amount of foreign reserves. This is due to the fact that it relies greatly on oil exports. If the price of oil in the World Market drops, the country may suffer. By amassing large amounts of foreign currencies, the government can cushion the economy.

As of February 2020, the Forex reserves of the USA totaled $129 billion. Similar to other countries of the world, Russia also holds reserve assets in USD. However, they also keep some gold. The price of an ounce of gold often relies on its intrinsic value. If Russia's economy declines, gold won't be enough to support the country's stability.

Besides, gold is only worth the amount the buyer is willing to pay for it. During a market crash, recession, or inflation, the mechanics of supply and demand determine the value of precious metals.

How Can Banks Intervene with Forex Rates

Central banks have the power to influence foreign exchange rates. The member countries of the European Union (EU) agreed to maintain a band around target exchange rates.

When necessary, they will implement this monetary policy through intervention in Forex markets. Even without exchange rate commitments, Japan and the United States often intervene in global FX markets in order to stabilize the value of their domestic currency.

Central banks can use a "foreign exchange intervention" as a monetary policy device. When a central bank influences a currency's funds transfer rate, they do so using their asset reserves or their authority to generate banknotes and coinage.

More often than not, central banks in developing countries intervene in Forex markets so that they could build reserves for themselves. Or, they provide for another country's national banks to stabilize exchange rates.

Stabilization invites traders to place investments on a particular nation or Forex market. It makes them feel comfortable with the exchanges that are going to transpire on the marketplace. Currency stabilization requires both long-term and short-term interventions. Destabilizing effects may come from both non-market or market forces.

When a central financial institution increases the amount of money circulating within an economy, extra care is needed to reduce its inadvertent effects like hyperinflation.

The efficacy of a Forex intervention relies heavily on how the organization central to the policy mitigates the consequences of the intervention.

In implementing an intervention, central banks face three challenges:

- The number of reserve assets of a country

- The economic issues faced by the government

- The volatile market conditions of the Forex exchanges associated with the nation

Often, after the execution of monetary policies, a corrective intervention may be required. This is done to fix and mitigate the consequences and issues that resulted from the initial intervention of the central bank.

Forex intercessions come in two types:

1. The government or central agency assesses its currency When the financial organization determines that the value of the domestic currency is too high for the economies of other countries, especially those that import their products or goods,

2. the central bank of the country in question or another nation will definitely intervene.

3.　　Their fiat currency should be affordable for their major consumers.

Hence, even though the majority of the world's currencies are floating, there are instances wherein a central agency needs to control or bolster the value of their currency. The only currency that can be considered pure, in terms of being tarnished with repeated interventions, is the CAD. As stated before, the Canadian government had not intervened with the exchange rate of their legal tender in the last forty years.

For example, from the end of Q3 2011 to the start of Q1 2015, the Swiss National Bank (SNB) set a minimum exchange rate between the Euro and Swiss Franc. This prevented the Swiss franc from increasing beyond a level at which their major importers couldn't afford their Swiss goods.

For more than three years, this proved to be advantageous for Switzerland and its importers. However, the Swiss National Bank determined that it must let the Swiss Franc to freely float. Without warning other countries, they released the minimum exchange rate.

2.　　The intervention is a short-term response to an economic or political event

Often, an event can make a country's currency move in a specific direction over a short period. In this case, a central bank will try to reduce the market's volatility and provide liquidity through intervention.

After the SNB allowed their currency to stay afloat, the Swiss franc decreased in value by approximately twenty-five percent. After this, the SNB implemented a corrective intervention to mitigate the volatility.

On paper, Forex interventions can sometimes be risky. Set monetary policies can even undermine the credibility of a bank when it can't maintain stability.

Defending the domestic currency from speculators was the cause of the economic crisis in Mexico in 1994. A similar event also happened in Thailand, which sparked the 1997 Asian Financial Crisis.

Chapter 4:

What Factors Drive the Forex Market?

Foreign exchanges are global marketplaces wherein sellers and buyers from all around the world participate in currency trading. Nowadays, Forex trading is considered a global phenomenon. Macroeconomics, the component of economics that is concerned with general or large-scale economic factors, such as national productivity and interest rates, affects exchange rates.

Macroeconomic statistics, like inflation, greatly impact Forex markets. Commodity, bond, and stock markets also influence exchange rates; surpluses, trade deficits, and other international trade numbers play a major role in exchange rates and price action. At times, political news can even change the rates of affected currency pairs.

Overarching macroeconomic factors drive foreign exchanges. The factors that are discussed in this chapter can influence your decision and help you estimate the value of a domestic currency at any point in the future. A country's economic and political status play a great part in the fluctuation of exchange rates.

The economic health of a nation can change in no time. The same thing can be said to currency values and exchange rates.

They are all affected by the factors below. Remember that the majority of successful Forex traders are well disciplined. And, they stick to trading rules, which are governed by elements that have a significant effect on the market and its constituents.

Today, Forex traders and investors don't need to stick to popular currencies only, in order to gain high profits.

Inflation Rates

As mentioned in the previous chapters, inflation causes changes in exchange rates, increases unemployment rate, and prompts governments to devalue their currency. On the contrary, a nation with a low inflation rate experiences currency appreciation. This implies that the value of its domestic currency is rising. The countries with a high inflation rate have high-interest rates and see currency depreciation.

Interest Rates

Like inflation, changes in or the fluctuation of interest rates within a country also affect exchange rates and currency values. When this stat increases, the value of the currency of the country in question improves as well. This is due to the fact that high-interest rates also provide high profits for lenders. Lenders from other nations will be enticed to invest in the country, provide foreign capital, and lend money.

Inflation, Forex rates, and interest rates are correlated with each other.

Foreign capital, in particular, can increase a currency's value.

B.O.P.

The currency account of a country and its earnings reflect on its net exports (commercial balance). This contains the total transaction count and the country's debt, imports, and exports. A deficit in its current account can cause depreciation. Depreciation can also occur when imports exceed exports, liabilities exceed assets, or expenses exceed revenues.

A surplus is the exact opposite of a deficit. If a country spends more money on imports than on exports, the domestic currency may depreciate.

B.O.P. or Balance of Payments can cause the exchange rate of a domestic currency to fluctuate. Under a fiat currency exchange system, supply and demand drive the relationship between exchange rates and balance of payments.

The Mechanics of Supply and Demand

In a floating market, crowd psychology and the interaction between sellers and buyers determine the rates and prices. The number of buyers represent the demand for a specific instrument, product, or commodity.

On the other hand, the sellers and the amount of security they are offering symbolize the supply in the market. If these two elements remain in balance, then the price of the security or commodity in question will be largely unchanged for some time.

However, if the relationship becomes imbalanced, then the price will either rise or fall. When the demand surpasses the supply, the number of buyers exceeds the number of sellers. In this case, prices will rise. This tempts fresh sellers to sell their products or assets.

Conversely, if the supply surpasses the demand, then there are more sellers than buyers. In this case, prices decrease to a point where the number of buyers increases, and prospects are turned to paying customers.

Price formation on any market is governed by the relationship between supply and demand. They represent the market sentiment and the number of sellers and buyers on the market.

In terms of the law of supply and demand in foreign exchanges, macro- and micro-economics and levels of support resistance are involved. Traders use price charts and technical analyses, which have been developed to capture and highlight future price points.

At the macro-level, the law of supply and demand covers the availability of domestic currencies.

Wholesale supplies are also largely involved.

Historically, the purchasing power of a currency is affected when the country issuing it increases the number of banknotes in circulation.

The government may do this to meet its obligations. This happened in Germany. To pay deficits and war reparations, Germany printed more banknotes than the number of what was allowed by its monetary policies.

As a result, the value of the Reichsmark fell. The excess supply of the currency created an excess demand for services and goods.

Over time, the purchasing power of the currency eroded.

The law of demand and supply is also considered a theory. It explains the relationship between the sellers of a security or commodity and the buyers of the resource. The law also explains the factors that affect the interactions between the buyers and sellers.

In global markets, demand and supply pull each other down. When the supply reaches a certain level, it will decrease and demand will increase, and vice versa. Nevertheless, several factors affect both demand and supply.

The following factors can either decrease or increase supply or demand in one way or the other.

-       Movement vs. Shifts

In economics, the "shifts" and "movements," in the context of the law of supply and demand curves, represent different market phenomena. What does this mean?

A movement refers to a change in a demand curve. It signifies changes in the quantity and price of a security or currency.

On the curve, the quantity is based on the distance between two points. A movement implies that the relationship between the demand and the quantity of a product is inconsistent.

Hence, a movement occurs when the price or the number of sellers of a given currency changes. The demanded quantity changes as well. Simply put, a slight or noticeable movement along the curve only appears when a price change causes a change in the demanded quantity.

The same thing can be said of any movement along a supply curve. The quantity supplied describes the number of goods, securities, or services supplied at a given price in a market.

When a price change causes a change in the quantity supplied, a movement appears along the supply curve.

In contrast, a shift appears along a supply or demand curve when the quantity supplied or demanded changes even when the price remains the same. For example, if 1 Swiss franc (CHF) was equivalent to 1.03 USD and the demand for the first currency

increased from Q2 to Q3, a shift could be seen along the given supply curve.

That implies that the initial curve changed. This happens when a certain factor affected the quantity supplied, while the price remains unchanged. Conversely, if the exchange rate of the Swiss franc against the USD was 1.02 and the quantity supplied decreased from Q2 to Q3 2017, then a shift could be observed.

- Equilibrium price

The equilibrium price is also referred to as the market-clearing price in which the quantity demanded is equivalent to the quantity supplied. On a graph, this is the point where the supply and demand curves intersect. It's the price whereat the seller can offer all the units he/she wants and the buyer can purchase all the units he/she wants.

The supply curve is a graphical representation of the relationship between the cost of a security and the quantity supplied for a given period. The price is located on the left vertical axis.

The quantity appears on the horizontal axis.

On any day that the quantity supplied is fixed, the curve is just a vertical line.

- More factors that affect supply

Production capacity and costs, including materials and labor expenses, as well as the total number of competitors, affect how much supply is needed in finance markets. Ancillary factors, like availability, material, weather, and supply chain reliability, can also affect supply.

- More factors that affect demand

Market sentiment, consumer preferences, shifts, and substitute availability directly affect demand for a particular product.

For instance, if the value of a major currency drops, then the demand for that currency will rise in Forex markets.

On the one hand, high pricing will attract sellers. As the market becomes saturated with supply, new sellers will decrease their prices.

Low prices attract customers. This increases demand, and the cycle continues.

In conclusion, the law of supply states that low prices are associated with high supply. This triggers prospects to make purchases. The law of demand states that high prices attract sellers and discourage would-be clients to buy the security or product in question.

You can use the law of supply and demand to determine actual market prices and the volume of a financial instrument. As a whole, supply and demand interact with each other, and together, they can influence price and quantity.

Government Debt

Public debt is also known as national or government debt. A country buried in debt will find it hard to entice investors and acquire foreign capital. When numerous investors pull their money from a country in a given period, the inflation rate in that country will rise. If a market predicts that the government debt of a country is high, then the investors will sell their shares in open markets.

Developing countries usually engage in deficit financing in order to pay for government funding and public sector projects. This does stimulate the economy, but countries with large government debts and deficits are unattractive to investors. What's the reason for this? The answer is inflation. When inflation is high, the central bank of the country will pay off its deficits with cheap money at some point in the future.

If worse comes to worst, the government may urge its central bank to increase the number of banknotes circulating in the economy. The central governing body will do this in order to pay a huge percentage of the country's debt.

As stated before, currency devaluation causes hyperinflation. If the country can't pay its deficits by increasing the number of printed money or by selling domestic bonds, then it must offer its assets to foreigners or domestic corporate giants.

Doing so can increase prices and lower the value of the domestic currency.

Moreover, having a large deficit discourages foreign investors because they may think that the country may disregard its financial obligations in the future. They will be hesitant to own securities that are denominated in the country's fiat money.

All of these show that debt rating is an important determinant of the purchasing power and exchange rate of a domestic currency.

Terms of Trade

Associated with B.O.P. and current accounts, terms of trade are the relationship between the export prices to import prices. A nation's terms of trade are improved by an increase in its export prices. Of course, this bolsters the value of the domestic currency.

The Future Path of Interest Rates

With the exchange rates of currencies, they are expected to reflect a return. The returns are the interest rates.

Headline interest rates form the nominal return of the currency.

International investments, on the other hand, are only focused on realistic returns. What does this mean?

The real return is computed by subtracting the nominal return from the current inflation rate of the given country. Inflation erodes the value of a currency as time passes by.

Hence, interest rates must be above or equal to the inflation rate in order for the currency to retain its original value.

In first world countries, most central banks are decentralized. They act independently and are free from a government that provides a system of policy goals.

Central banks set monetary policies to achieve their targets. These include keeping inflation rate low and creating employments.

Often, central banks communicate their intentions and targets to the foreign exchange market.

Investors utilize this data in order to predict the future path of interest rates. They also use it to compare two or more predictions.

Doing so enables them and the markets to come up with an opinion and choose a position. The exchange rate is based on the relative values of the two currencies involved in the predictions.

The yield curve describes the assumed paths of interest rates.

Always remember that your perceptions and the yield curve should be drawn based on the changes in the interest rates.

Economic Performance and Political Stability

A nation's economic performance and political state directly affect the strength or the purchasing power of its currency.

A country with a stable government and economy entice foreign investors. Stability strengthens the economy and increases the value of the domestic currency.

If a country has fair trading policies, a strong economy, and less political turmoil, then its currency is very competitive in the Forex market and only experiences appreciation.

Speculation

If the purchasing power of a currency is forecasted to rise, traders and speculators will buy a lot. This increases the demand for that currency. Hence, the exchange rate will also rise because of high demand.

Deflections and Variations in an Economy's Macro-Economic Data

Macroeconomic events and data are the moving forces of Forex markets.

Nowadays, there is economic information created for DMA trading, currency trading, and stock investing.

The internet and direct market access (DMA) trading are closely related to each other.

Economic news from well-established media publishing economies, such as the NYTimes and The Balance, can move foreign exchange markets. They can also affect the strength of major currencies, like the JPY, USD, and EUR.

If you depend on technical analysis in making predictions, then you must look at and consider the latest or the upcoming key dates on your macroeconomic calendar. Those are the dates when there could be price fluctuations.

Keep in mind that those deviations can be trading opportunities. Such calendars rank news and economic releases by their market volatility or impact. The higher the impact or volatility that is associated with the economic release, the more important that data is to investors and traders.

Tailor-made ranking systems emphasize immediate prices impacts, instead of long-term effects. They suit traders who favor leveraging over other trading styles.

However, studying deviations and variations on economic calendars rather than using technical analysis fits investors who have resided in a place with a shorter time zone than the country where the base currency is issued in.

With the number of weekly economic news releases, investors have to design strategies that enable them to analyze large data in a short period.

To do this, they often take note of deviation levels from past data points and information that is consistent in different economic news.

They also consider the forecasts of well-known financial analysts, like Meredith Whitney and Abby Joseph Cohen.

Recession

As mentioned in chapter 2, a recession can greatly impact exchange rates. When a nation sees a recession, unemployment rates will rise, and interest rates will fall.

Plus, recession causes economic instability, and at times, it can even lessen exports and imports. A recession can also force a government that is buried in debt to devalue its domestic currency.

Credit ratings

Macroeconomic news and forecasts provide traders and speculators a general overview of the status and health of an economy and the strength of its currency.

The profile created from collected data directly feeds the assumptions for the future paths of interest rates. This is a factor that can greatly influence currency price information.

Furthermore, the exchange rate of a currency can also be used to gauge the market sentiment in an economy.

In other words, an economic profile can determine how much confidence buyers have in a particular currency's ability to perform on foreign exchanges.

It can also determine the capability of an economy to fulfill its obligations. Can it lower its deficits in the future? Will the country be further buried in debt?

A nation's obligations include servicing, repayment of government debts, and public provisions like pensions, benefits, education, healthcare, etc.

In that regard, economies are like households or individuals. When people apply for a long-term mortgage, a short-term loan, or a credit card, the lender assesses their creditworthiness.

They do so before providing access to funds. They check the borrower's assets, overheads, savings, disposable income, and current salaries, before making a judgment.

The summation of the aforementioned criteria creates an individual's credit rating. The credit rating measures the capability of the borrower to pay off his/her debt. It also quantifies the belief of the lender that he/she will receive full repayment and the interest due.

The higher the credit score is, the stronger the level of trust that the lender has on the borrower. The same can be said at an economic or state level.

Brokers, banks, and rating agencies assess a country's finances and the deviations in its economic data before providing a loan. This determines the economy's credit risk and credit score.

The AAA rating is the best rating for any country striving to empower its currency and economy.

The triple-A suggests that lending millions of dollars to the country in question is risk-free.

Switzerland has had a triple-A rating for the last three decades. This is why the Swiss franc is a highly coveted currency, as much as the US dollar.

The CHF is viewed as a financial refuge. This is because of the stability of Switzerland's economy, financial system, and government. The high buying interest of the franc causes its value to soar.

Earlier, you learned that you can use a yield curve to map interest rates, which can negatively or positively affect the value of a currency. A good credit rating implies low-interest rates that signify low rewards to investors of the local currency.

Price formation in the Forex market makes use of the two opposing forces since both are sensitive to deviations.

Chapter 5

Techniques to Trading Forex

The foreign exchange market is open 5 days a week and 24 hours a day. Different types of currencies are traded on major financial centers such as Australia, London, Tokyo, and New York. According to Bloomberg Businessweek, an American business magazine, there is always a global Forex market open somewhere. When you consider time zones, it implies that there are currency buyers and sellers 24/7.

As stated, there are as many currencies as the total number of countries worldwide. Currencies are always traded in pairs. When the first one is sold, the second is bought. Take exchanging your USD for EUR as an example. In this case, the currency pair is EUR/USD. Traders use techniques, which are known as Forex analyses, in determining price action and the strength of each currency.

For example, if a financial analyst expects the EUR to rise against the USD, then traders will purchase Euros using British pounds. If the GBP will rise against the EUR, then they will offer EUR/GBP. Remember that when the value of the base currency increases relative to the quote currency, then the rate of exchange is increasing. If the value of the first currency rises relative to the fall of the quote, then the exchange rate decreases.

Forex analyses examine and scan the deviation in the prices of currency pairs.

The primary goal of these techniques is to isolate future price movements. In FX markets, the major aim of traders and investors is to make a profit from buying and selling currencies.

Banks, traders, hedge funds, commercial companies, and investment management companies utilize one or more types of forex analysis. They do this to determine the best deals for a currency pair at any particular time.

Forex analysis can be done manually or automatically. Like humans, computers could analyze trends and historical data if properly programmed.

The most effective techniques for Forex trading are dependent on the individual or entity making the trade. The trading strategy could either be fundamental or technical in nature. In most cases, financial analysts are concerned with the economic health of the country that issues the currency they're observing.

They also consider the factors that could affect exchange rates and the effect of the rise or fall of that domestic currency to others. Overall, they focus on price patterns and price movements. Always remember this when you're conducting a technical or fundamental analysis.

Statistical and sentimental approaches fall under either of the two types. The statistical approach can include finding tendencies or patterns within technical or fundamental data.

On the other hand, sentiment analysis involves crowd psychology, trader perceptions, or their positions. Both can help determine the health of a price trend. The price trend is the momentum and direction of the price of a currency.

As a trader, you should use a type of Forex analysis when making buy or sell decisions. Technical analysis can be fundamental or technical in nature. You can either use charting tools, news-based events, or economic indicators.

Here are the two types of Forex analysis you should use and know about:

The Fundamental Approach

Technical analysis involves studying charts to determine trends or patterns. Fundamental analysis, on the other hand, includes the perusal of news headlines and the analysis of economic data reports. It is a method used for analyzing social, political, and economic forces that influence currency exchange rates.

The fundamental analysis primarily utilizes the mechanism of supply and demand in determining a currency pair's past, present, and future exchange rates. It also involves the analysis of the factors that affect the determinants.

Simply put, in this approach, you must study different factors to ascertain what economy sucks, and what is thriving.

Understanding the reasons behind the occurrence of certain events is integral in fundamental analysis. How do unemployment rates of a nation affect its economy and monetary policy? What are the factors that affect the level of demand of the domestic currency?

Fundamental analysts propose that a good economy has a strong currency.

For example, the value of the GBP has strengthened because the economy of the United Kingdom has improved.

As the economy improves, increasing interest rates may be required in order to manage inflation and growth. Plus, high-interest rates make GBP-denominated assets attractive to foreign investors.

For them to acquire such financial assets, investors and traders need to purchase some British pounds first. Accordingly, GBP's value and its exchange rate will increase.

When using fundamental analysis, you must understand how political, financial, and economic news can impact future exchange rates. Just remember that fundamental analysis is dependent or should be based on the weakness or strength of a nation's economic outlook.

The Technical Approach

The technical approach is a currency trading discipline used for evaluating investments and identifying trading opportunities. This can be done through the analysis of statistical and graphical trends collected from trading activities, such as volume and price movement.

Technical analysis can be in the form of an automated or manual system. Typically, a manual system involves a trader.

He/she analyzes indicators and interpreting data in order to make an effective buy or sell decision. Whereas, an automated system involves a trader that is teaching a program to study indicators, look for specific signals, and execute effective buy or sell decisions.

Either way, Forex systems utilize past price actions in order to determine the future movements of a currency.

• At a glance

Technical analysis is the foundation wherein traders study price action and movement. Economists and analysts also consider it a theory. It states that an individual should look at price movements when determining future price movements and present trading conditions.

Anyone who utilizes this approach is referred to as a technical analyst. Any trader who uses technical analysis is called "technical trader."

Theoretically, all present market data can be seen in the exchange rates.

In most cases, the axiom of technical traders is "It is all in the charts." This implies that all of the data they need is reflected in the charts, charted indexes, and past and present market prices.

Since price represents all the data needed, price action is what you need to make a trading decision. Technical analysis basically looks at the flow, trends, and rhythm in price actions. As mentioned in chapter 2, "history will repeat itself."

This age-old adage also applies in currency trading, and it's what the technical approach is all about.

If a past rate was held as a noteworthy resistance or support level, traders would consider it and base their decisions around that particular turning point.

They also look for similar trends and patterns formed in the past and base their trades from historical patterns.

Technical analysis is more about probability than predictions. In the most essential respects, the technical approach is the study of historical trends and price action for the purpose of identifying patterns and determining probabilities of future price movements.

So, here's the million-dollar question?

How can you study and analyze historical price actions?

In the trading world, when you say "I use technical analysis," the first thing that comes to the mind of seasoned traders is a chart.

Analysts and Forex traders utilize charts to easily visualize relevant past trading data.

By studying past data, you can spot patterns and trends. As currency traders look for specific chart patterns and price levels, these patterns will start to manifest themselves.

However, just because Jerry and James are studying the same indicators or chart, it doesn't' mean that they will have the same idea and hypothesis about future price action. Contrary to its name, technical analysis is quite subjective. The most important thing is you understand turning points, Bollinger Bands, or Fibonacci levels.

• The price scales

Fundamental analysis focuses on the statistical analysis of price movements. The interpretation of a chart varies among currency traders, and also, the majority of brokerage and online charting programs of today display chart styles differently. The two most used price scales in technical analysis for currency trading are the following:

- Logarithmic price scale

This is also referred to as log and is dependent on the rate of change in the value of the currency in question. On the y-axis or vertical axis, logs represent price spacing. The logarithmic price scale is often the standard chart style in online trading platforms.

- Linear price scale

Like the former, the arithmetic price scale also represents prices on the vertical axis. It uses equidistant spacing to display absolute values and designated prices.

The majority of technical traders utilize logarithmic price scales. These are plotted so that the values aren't positioned equidistantly. Rather, the points are plotted in a way wherein two percent changes have the same vertical distance on the logarithmic scale.

Equal spaces between the points in the chart represent recurring percent changes. For example, the amount of space between 20 USD and 40 USD is the same as the distance between 40 USD and

80 USD. This is because both cases represent a 100% price increase.

In a linear price scale, movements are not related to percent changes. Instead, price changes are plotted with each unit of change that is in accordance with a constant unit value. In an arithmetic chart, each value change is persistent on the scale.

In contrast with a logarithmic price scale, an arithmetic chart can easily be drawn manually. Often, Forex traders use this technique in short-term currency exchanges.

Other than the scales, technical analysis is also based on two fundamental assumptions.

These serve as the foundations of technical trading and have shaped its framework.

-       Markets stay efficient. They are composed of values that represent factors, which influence a currency's value.

-       Most random market price movements move in notable and identifiable trends and patterns. These patterns and trends are repeated at varying intervals.

•   The underlying assumptions

Charles Dow, the co-founder of the Wall Street Journal, one of the most respected financial publications in the world, released several editorials that explained the technical analysis theory. He invented the Dow Jones Industrial Average (DJIA), which is also known as the Dow.

The field of technical analysis is based on his works and assumptions:

- The world's Forex and stock markets discount everything Technical analysts believe that everything from a financial organization's market factors to crowd market psychology is included or can be read on price changes on a scale. In a technical approach, the analysis of price movements is seen as the result of the demand and supply for a specific currency or stock.

- Prices move in patterns and trends

Prices and exchange rates exhibit trends over time or even in a short-term period. Most stock prices seldom move erratically. Rather, they often just continue a historical trend. Most technical currency trading strategies revolve around this conjecture of Dow.

- History will repeat itself

Price movements and price actions are repetitive in nature. The primary cause of this is crowd psychology. Overselling is one effect of negative market sentiment. Do recall that the overselling of stocks caused the Great Depression of the 1930s. And, the overselling of subprime mortgages caused the Great Recession in 2008.

Market psychology can be predictable since it's based on emotions, such as excitement or fear.

Hence, it also affects the points and data on a chart.

In general, you can use technical analysis to visualize repetitive price movements, to understand trends, and to analyze the sentiments and emotions behind each major price change.

- How to use technical analysis

With technical analysis, you can forecast the market movement of tradable instruments. These include commodities and currency pairs since they are also affected by the mechanism of supply and demand. The same thing goes for futures, bonds, and stocks.

In truth, some economists just view "the technical approach" as the study of supply and demand. Generally, this technique is used to analyze price changes. But, some people also use this approach to track numbers and the following statistics:

- Resistance and support levels

- Moving averages
- Oscillators
- Momentum and volume indicators
- Chart patterns
- Price trends

When reading charts, you may use the guide below.

1. Recall Dow's assumptions and base your readings on any of his three conjectures.

2.   Choose a specific time frame.

3.   Read one or more charts to spot patterns and trends.

4.   Look at support and resistance levels.

5.   Consider the volume of trades.

6.   Utilize moving averages in filtering small-scale price fluctuations.

7.   Use oscillators and indicators to support your insights.

Techniques Beginners Can Use to Trade Forex

•   Come to understand the drivers

To become a successful trader, you have to understand the relationships that exist between markets and the factors that drive these links. Doing so allows you to know where certain factors root from and what drives them.

For instance, investors see the recovery of a stock market as a sign of economic recovery. They believe that companies in that country would have to improve their earnings.

Therefore, stocks would rise and their worth would increase. If great valuations are expected in the future, then it's advised to trade today.

As a currency trader, you shouldn't just focus on the Forex markets. Although you don't intend to invest in stocks, bonds, or commodities, looking at charts associated with the indexes in other markers is a good way to predict future price movements.

- Chart Indexes

Unlike other techniques, charting indexes is relatively easy. You just have to chart integral indexes for a market for a specific period. Doing so can help you know the drivers in that market and the relationships that exist between each factor.

For instance, in 2009, the value of gold increased to record highs. This could have been due to the fact that during the time, the value of major and minor currencies were falling. Or, the value of cheap USD fueled a boom in commodities and demand. In any case, speculations drove market movements.

- Find similar trends in other markets

In chapter 2, it's clearly stated that stock markets affect foreign exchanges. The increase in the production of a particular product or commodity can also influence other markets.

High demand for a particular product under a brand could increase the share prices of the company or corporation that owns the name.

When this happens, the trend can affect the exchange rate between specific pairs.

Even commodities, including wheat, gold, and oil, can impact the rates of exchange between nations. Nonetheless, price shifts of a commodity won't affect all countries.

By charting other securities and financial instruments on a regular basis, you will see whether the markets involved have similar trends or not. From here, you could take advantage of the similarity.

If you think the value of JPY will increase due to a sudden decrease in the value of Nikkei stocks, then sell your Japanese yens. Wait for the turning point and pour all your JPYs in the market. Trade it with a currency that you think could give you a high profit in the future.

Here's another example. If the USD/JPY pair signifies an oversold position, then the BOJ will intervene to devalue the Japanese yen. When this happens, Japanese exports and the share prices of large Asian conglomerates could be affected. The devaluation will weaken the value of the yen, but it will help in the recovery of the economy.

In most cases, when an economy recovers, the purchasing power of the domestic currency also rises. Hence, the cycle continues. It's up to traders like you when to buy or sell the currency in Forex markets.

- Time your trades

Remember that timing your trades is crucial in winning big in Forex.

By finding the tuning points on both shorter and longer time frames, you can fine-tune your transactions and end up with a successful trade.

You can place your first trade at the double bottom or Fibonacci level indicated on long-term charts. The Fibonacci levels are horizontal lines on charts. They indicate where resistance or support level may occur. Each Fibonacci level is associated with a percentage.

The percentage represents the difference between a reversal and retracement. In Forex, you will often encounter retracements. A price retracement is any temporary reversal of a quote within a notable price trend.

If your first trade fails, then time your second one on a pullback or on the support level.

Discipline, preparation, and patience will distinguish you from investors who trade on impulse. Without proper preparation and the analysis of FX indicators, it can be hard to earn large profits in the Forex markets. This maxim stays true even if your capital is worth several thousands of dollars.

Acquiring Strategies and Forex Trading Systems

You can either manually apply your preferred trading system or use an automated forex trading strategy. An automated system can incorporate fundamental and technical analysis into your trading decisions with ease. For this to happen, you may code a program, hire someone to do the coding for you, or purchase a software product.

Automated Forex trading will enable you to step away from cumbersome manual trades. A program that is tailor-made to analyze trends, deviations, and turning points can set parameters for currency trading. If you prefer automating your trades, you can either use a free software or buy a licensed program.

If you know how to code or know someone who can do so, then it will be best to develop a program that matches your trading preferences.

If you feel that your approaches are quite lacking and you want a more-reassuring trading technique, then purchase an application online.

Make sure that it features multiple trading systems.

Numerous manual trading systems and automated technical approaches can be purchased online. ZapMeta and AdmiralMarkets are only two of the hundreds of websites that offer effective trading strategies.

All in all, no best method exists for currency trading since the factors that drive the market and the value of the currencies are ever- changing.

A single economic trend could change the movement of prices in foreign exchanges.

A whim of a nation's leader could raise tariffs and ratify strict trade policies.

This could cause the depreciation of another nation's fiat money.

Moreover, the market itself and the currencies in the world are all volatile even with their liquidity.

You can spend an entire day ruminating about all the effects of the factors that affect the exchange rate.

Nevertheless, the most feasible strategy for any trader depends and should be based on his/her time frame and on accurate, relevant economic information.

If you're a short-term trader, then you must focus on real-time and recent economic data. As it is, technical analysis, instead of a fundamental approach, could be right for you.

Conversely, long-term traders with access to historical economic data often choose fundamental analysis.

Chapter 6

What Risks Are There When Trading Forex?

Now that you know the best trading strategies for Forex trading, it's time to be aware of the hidden dangers that are lurking in the market. In the FX market, it's relatively easy to enter deals and trade currencies. A mobile device or personal computer and a decent internet connectivity are the basic things you need to start trading. However, experience, trading knowledge, and awareness of the risks are necessary if you want to win big in currency trading.

• Interest rate risk

The fluctuations in interest rates can significantly impact the exchange rate of a domestic currency. When interest rates increase, the exchange rate rises as well.

A stable domestic currency generates high returns and attracts foreign investors.

In contrast, the currency depreciates when interest rates decrease. This prompts investors to resell their stocks and convert their assets denominated in that currency.

With this relationship, the differential between the two currencies can create fluctuations in the exchange rate. Typically, the pair with the highest interest rates attracts the most attention.

• Counterparty risk

In foreign exchanges, the counterparty is the entity or platform where you open and close positions. In other words, they are the broker, dealer, or brokerage platform.

As such, this risk refers to the defaults of the platform or broker in transactions. Counterparty risk may have roots from threats of bankruptcy or lack of regulation. You will pour your money onto your account on the platform in the hopes of gaining profits from currency trading. This is the reason why you should only create a trading account with a trusted and reliable broker. The organization or platform must be regulated by a regulatory body.

Nowadays, it can't be denied that there are numerous scam websites out there. So you should be vigilant and careful when choosing a broker. You mustn't only choose one that fits your trading style, but you must also select a well-known and long-standing entity, firm, or broker.

If the counterparty doesn't pay you, then you can say goodbye to your money. Also, if the entity becomes bankrupt or is poorly regulated, you may not be able to recover your money in your trading account.

How can you avoid being a victim of such scams?

Always check the "About page" of the broker. Check how long they've been in business and their regulatory number. You should also check online reviews about their reputation.

The entity should be registered and regulated in the country where its headquarters is located.

The Autorité des Marchés Financiers (AMF) is the regulatory commission in France. In the United Kingdom, the Financial Conduct Authority, which is more commonly known as FCA, regulates brokerage platforms there. The regulatory body in the United States is the US Securities and Exchange Commission (SEC). In Australia, it's the Australian Securities and Investments Commission (ASIC).

Make sure that the platform that you will trust with your money is regulated by any of the aforementioned agencies. To check the company's affiliation, look for their registration number on their website. And, enter the numbers on the website of the agency that regulates them.

Other than those, the counterparty should be considered strong financially. This means that it should be well-established, has a good reputation, and will not go bankrupt in the near future.

Lastly, you must also look at the number of its Monthly Active Users (MAU).

With this key performance indicator, you can estimate how many active sellers or buyers are on the platform daily.

- Country risk

Aside from counterparty and interest rate risks, you should also consider the political and economic stability of the issuing country.

This is the danger of trading minor currencies. Traders refer to this as country risk.

Developing countries, such as Pakistan and Croatia, have their domestic currencies pegged to one of the major currencies. These include the USD or GBP. The central bank of the country regulates its reserve assets in order to stabilize the exchange rate.

However, because of BOP, the domestic currency could weaken, and the government would be forced to devalue its fiat money.

Remember that devaluation can negatively or positively affect the value of a currency. In this case, the said monetary policy is for the payments of outstanding deficits. If it isn't for bolstering the country's exports, then it can cause inflation and weaken the currency.

If you don't follow price signals, you may face problems with bankruptcy and liquidity.

A currency crisis can worsen the risk, devaluation, and liquidity problems especially when FX trading is concerned.

- Liquidity risk

When it comes to size and liquidity, the foreign exchange market is the largest worldwide. Its inflated liquidity enables investors to easily open and close positions in the market. This means that you can find sellers and buyers of specific pairs with relative ease. Its high liquidity also implies that traders will seldom face a shortage of supply and demand for a specific currency.

In addition to that, currency prices won't be much affected because of the stability of the market. Low liquidity can increase asset prices.

Even though this is the case, the Forex market isn't exempted from periods of low liquidity. Do recall that most foreign exchanges are closed during holidays and weekends. During such periods, brokers raise the size of their spreads. They try to increase their commission per transaction since there are fewer traders on such occasions than on regular days.

When trading costs increase, brokers will offer variable spreads. Variable spreads change based on existing trading and market conditions. As a beginner, you should only go for fixed spreads. If you don't know how a particular pair behaves, opt for option number two.

- Leverage risk

Leveraging in the Forex market is utilized to increase returns.

However, it can also lead to great losses. This is one of the major risks associated with Forex. Due to price fluctuations, the broker may issue a margin call. What is this?

A margin call is a demand by a broker that you must deposit more securities or cash to cover possible losses on their side. In other words, you'll be required to pay the additional margin. The higher the amount you've invested, the greater your potential losses will be.

- Transaction risks

The difference in time between the opening and closing of a transaction creates possible transaction risk. Errors in confirmation, handling, and communication can also lead to issues, complaints, and losses. Since currency trading requires planning within 24 hours, the rate of exchange often changes before the position closes. The longer you hold a position, the more money you will lose.

- Political risk

In the past, some of President Trump's tweets have affected the stock and Forex markets. Some financial analysts observed that his tweets created short-term volatility in 2017. In 2018, his activities on Twitter affected the share prices of Boeing, Toyota, General Dynamics, and Lockheed Martin.

Furthermore, political events, including elections, make stock prices, and exchange rates unstable.

Since such events cause uncertainty, the investment environment in the country in question is negatively affected. Investors will be hesitant to place their money on the market. This makes markets volatile.

Scandals, protests, and strikes also create fluctuations in the price action and exchange rate of a specific currency pair. You can minimize risks by checking the latest political events in the countries involved with the pair you will order.

Chapter 7

How Can Beginners Manage the Risks Inherent in Forex Trading?

Forex trading is quite similar to stock investing. The higher the amount of money you invest, the greater your potential profit or loss will be. In currency trading, you need to invest to make a profit. Drawdowns—a decline in a fund or an investment—also happen in currency trading. If you have limited funds, losing a lot will make it hard for you to get back on track.

It is common for beginners to think that Forex trading is easy and fast. But, in truth, becoming good at trading currencies and making profitable trades require patience, knowledge, time, and commitment.

If you don't want to gamble in foreign exchanges, you have to manage the risks mentioned in the previous chapter. You also need to consider your broker's trading conditions.

Risk management is integral in Forex trading. The market is unpredictable. Risks can make you lose your capital.

Speculators are the most vulnerable to trading risks. This is because they tend to invest more than what they can afford.

The use of risk management in currency trading separates successful traders from the people who deplete their trading account. When you can manage existing trading risks properly, you can control the amount of capital you can lose on a Forex transaction. Even if you experience the worst-case scenario in a trade, you won't go bankrupt.

1.   Only invest your excess money

This is the very first unwritten rule in Forex trading. Only risk the money that you can afford to lose.

Many beginner traders believe that their first few trades will bring in extra cash.

However, like seasoned traders, beginners will experience losses if they trade carelessly.

If you trade using your monthly budget, stop right there! Forex trading is inherently risky. Don't take risks by using the money for your basic necessities.

2.   Your risk/reward ratio should be set at 1:3

The RRR is an essential tool in currency trading. As a Forex trader, you have to mitigate and eradicate downside risks.

The RRR helps you set your take-profit and stop-loss orders based on your preferred risk tolerance.

Although the ratio depends on every trader, the RRR of 1:3 is the most widely used. With this, you can earn three times as much as your capital.

For example, if the difference between your entry-level and stop-loss order is 20 pips and the distance between your Forex entry point and take-profit is 60 pips, then your risk\reward ratio is 1:3. This implies that you're willing to risk 20 pips to get 60 pips.

3.   Maintain the risks

If you can't completely eradicate a risk, then it's advised to just maintain it. The majority of beginners will increase their investments after making a profit in an earlier trade.

If luck is on your side, you can win big by risking everything. However, this is the best way of wiping your trading account clean.

Three winning streaks don't mean that your next trade will be successful. As a beginner, you have to study the trends, the price movement, and the reasons behind your success.

If you become an expert in predicting future prices, and you have an eight-five percent win-rate, only then should you try investing all of the funds in your trading account.

Beginners like yourself should always trade like you're making your first-ever Forex trade. Don't include your gains in your investment.

4.   Control and understand leverage

Foreign exchanges are leveraged markets. Because of margin trading and leveraging, you can borrow money more than your capital investment.

As collateral, the broker or financier will only ask you to set aside a small percentage of your entire trading account.

When leveraging, you'll make huge profits.

If you only make $30 per trade with your $500 trading account, you can earn $90 by borrowing

$1000. This strategy is best combined with the 1:3 RRR.

5.   Two percent investment

As a beginner, the best tactic you can do to manage the risks is to invest only a small percentage of your account on each transaction.

By doing so, you can avoid losing streaks and prevent a huge drawdown in your trading account.

This can kill your account, and make it difficult to reach breakeven. It's recommended to only trade two percent of your account.

Chapter 8

Beginner Mistakes to Avoid

Time and time again, currency trading is a risky activity. Other than effective risk management techniques, you also need to watch out for common pitfalls that a beginner trader like you could fall into.

Having the ability to see and avoid beginner mistakes when trading Forex can help in leveraging your account and make profits from a small amount.

Don't lose your capital just because you failed to avoid the most common mistake that beginners make when trading Forex.

1.   Trading without enough know-how about the FX market Currency trading is not like a walk in the park.

It will be for you only once you know the most common technical terms used by FX traders.

If you're a total newbie who doesn't even know the difference between the base and the quote of a currency pair, then don't trade because there's a high chance that you'll just lose your investment.

Watching a YouTube video about the Forex market doesn't make you an instant expert. Sure, the market is very enticing with the prospect of earning 15% - 20% of your investment per trade.

But, profiting that much requires prudence.

You have to choose a currency pair to trade, identify indicators, read historical data, study trends, etc. for you to win big in Forex trading.

2. Don't rely on your premonitions and presentiments

Your gut feeling isn't enough to make you earn high profits. You need an effective trading strategy for that to happen. Even gamblers use techniques to dominate rounds and bouts.

If you like reading charts, then use technical analysis to make a trading decision. If you prefer analyzing economic factors, such as GDP, interest rates, and unemployment rates, over making foresight, then choose fundamental analysis to dominate your trades.

3. Trading without considering risk management rules

In the last chapter, you learned how to manage risks in Forex trading. In your future trades, don't forget to incorporate those five tips into your game plan.

Plus, remember the additional tips below whenever you're trading currencies.

• Always take advantage of take-profit and stop-loss orders. This allows you to determine the amount of money you can lose in a trade.

• Set a maximum number of losses per week. If you lost all your profits and you only have your capital left, stop trading. Resume after a week or two because you may have missed an indicator that is affecting the pair you're trading.

• Don't change your risk level and risk\reward ratio just because you've profited from a few trades.

• Don't average down or up when the market is against your decisions.

4. Cut your losses

When you're losing money, the best thing to do is to stop trading. Many traders fail to do this. This is the main reason why they deplete their trading account.

They try to average up so that they could win back their losses But, by doing so, they only lose more.

The market won't instantly evolve. Some factors affect it, and indicators don't vanish within 24-hours.

If your capital keeps disintegrating after every trade, then cut your losses. Instead, formulate another trading strategy and analyze your resources again.

•

Chapter 9

Currency Pairs Explained

The quote or the second currency in a pair indicates the value needed to purchase one unit of the base currency. A currency pair compares the value of the base to the quote. 1.48/46 is an example of a Forex quote.

In the example, Euro and US dollars are being compared. The base is the Euro, while the quote is the US dollars. That Forex rate implies that you can buy 1 EUR for 1.48 USD.

An ISO currency code identifies a currency.

It contains three-letter alphabetic codes. When combined in pairs, they comprise the symbols and cross rates utilized in Forex trading.

Cross rates are important for traders who prefer to invest in a currency that is different from their country's fiat money. Often, FX traders utilize a cross rate to identify quotes that don't involve the USD.

In the next section, cross rates will be discussed further.

The ISO code for the US dollar is USD. The ISO code of a currency is composed of three uppercase letters. USD, JPY, CAD, and AUD are only some examples. When everything is taken into account, a currency pair is a quote of the exchange rate for two different currencies that are being traded in the market.

When ordering a currency pair, keep in mind that the base is bought while the quote is sold. The EUR/USD is considered the most liquid currency in the whole world, whereas the USD/JPY is the most popular pair.

Aside from trading currency pairs, the Forex market also allows the speculation and conversion of currencies for investment. All FX trades involve the purchasing of the base and the selling of the quote simultaneously.

Nevertheless, the base currency that has been bought using the second currency is often purchased as a "single" unit. Single units are also referred to as instruments that are sold or bought.

If you purchase a pair, you implicitly sell the quote and buy the base currency. The bid price stands for the amount of the second currency that you need in order to buy one unit of the base.

Conversely, if you sell a pair, you sell the base and receive the quote. The asking price represents the amount you'll receive for selling one unit of the base.

Unlike the commodity and stock market, the FX market allows you to trade currencies.

This means you sell one currency to purchase another. In stocks trading, you use cash to buy one share of Apple stock. Economic data relating to currency pairs—GDP information, interest rates, and economic announcements—affect the price of major currency pairs.

The EUR/USD (Euro against the US dollar) is a pair traded widely. As a matter of fact, it's considered the most liquid trading pair worldwide. This means you can convert it to cash easily and is available in all Forex trading platforms.

There are many trading pairs out there. The total number is almost as many as the number of currencies around the world.

As of date, approximately 180 legal currencies are circulating worldwide. Hence, it's possible to trade a single particular currency with 179 others. International FX brokers offer investors to trade in between forty to seventy currency pairs. The total number fluctuates since currencies and pairs come and go.

All trading pairs are grouped into major and minor currencies. The categorization depends on the volume of the trades that involve the currency pair. The most-traded currencies against the US dollar are considered as the major currencies. The major currency pairs are the USD/CAD, AUD/USD, USD/CHF, GBP/USD, USD/JPY, and EUR/USD.

The first two pairs are also referred to as the commodities currencies since Australia and Canada are rich in commodities. In addition to that, their prices affect both countries. The major pairs have liquid markers. Hence, trading for such pairs continues 24 hours a day 5 days a week. They also have narrow spreads.

Like other markets, the FX market has a spread. What's this? A spread is a bid. It's the price difference where an investor or trader can buy or sell an underlying asset. FX traders must know the spread in the Forex market they're trading on since the bid is the cost of each exchange. The broker is the one responsible for

 determining the bid and the charges. The charges, or the commission of the broker per trade, is included in the spread.

As an example, if you tend to make scalper (short-term) trades, then a high bid can result in the absorption of most of their profits. For those who are familiar with equities, the spread in a Forex transaction is the bid.

Exotic and Minor Pairs

The trading pairs that aren't associated with the US dollar, such as the EUR/CHF, GBP/JPY, and EUR/GBP, are called crosses or minor currencies. Crosses have wider spreads than major currencies. They're not as fluid as the major currencies. Nevertheless, they're often available in numerous Forex platforms.

The minor pairs that have the greatest volume among their group are the ones that have a major currency as their base.

The exotic pairs are only available in emerging markets. An emerging market can also be an emerging country.

It has the characteristics of a fully developed market, but it doesn't meet certain standards. The phrase "frontier market" is utilized for 2nd and 3rd world countries with riskier and smaller markets than an emerging country.

Emerging markets also have unique features. The structuring of their currency is different.

The USD, CAD, and JPY float freely and are independent. Emerging currencies are pegged or linked to a foreign currency, such as the Japanese Yen, Euro, or US dollar. The USD/SGD is an example of an exotic pair.

Knowing More About Cross Rates

As stated in the previous section, a cross rate is a currency exchange rate. The foreign exchange rate between the EUR and JPY can be considered a cross rate.

However, remember that a currency pair can only be considered a cross rate if the trader is not in any of the countries where the base and quote belong. Simply put, you can only consider a pair as a cross rate if you're currently residing in a location where neither the base nor the quote is being issued as the domestic currency.

Cross rates are often traded in the interbank spot foreign exchange market. To some degree, they're also exchanged in the options and forwards market. Minor cross rates are available in the interbank market. However, such pairs are less active than the major ones.

Without regard to whether or not the pair is traded, you can quote any base and quote against each other. You should quote cross rates that are similar in convention and value carefully, so you will avoid the beginner mistakes that new traders make.

For instance, you quote the NZD (New Zealand Dollar) at 1.05000 per AUD (Australian Dollar) in July 2016. Both currencies are quoted against the USD. When two currencies are traded near parity—the condition of being equal—you may misquote the base. If both are quoted against the USD, you'll find it hard to place the right bid since there's no guide in determining which the base is. In this case, the currency with a higher value than the other is considered as the base. If the NZD is being quoted against the AUD and both are cross-rates, it's typical to make the AUD as the base.

Major cross rates have wider spreads than the most popular USD- based pairs. This is due to the fact that in recent years, they've been actively quoted in interbank markets. The spreads in minor cross rates are wide as well. But, some aren't directly quoted at all. In this case, you should construct the quote based on the offers and bids in the component currencies versus the USD.

The markets where major crosses are traded are considered top- level Forex markets. Top-level Forex markets are where banks trade different currencies by dealing with another financial institution or through an online brokering platform.

Chapter 10

How to Choose the Best Currency Pairs to Trade

You now know the best trading strategies for your trading style and the risks and mistakes to avoid when trading currencies. So, it's time to pick the best currency pair for your trades. Should you choose the major pairs over the minor pairs? Will investing in an exotic pair bring you money?

Like copywriting, you have to find the right niche in currency trading. Think of every currency pair as a unique writing niche. Each set has its behavioral tendencies, which make it stand out from the rest. The same thing can be said of yourself. You're an exceptional individual, which implies that your trading style could be different from others.

When trading currencies, do match your behavior and personality with the currency pair that you're going to trade. Plus, you have to follow the magic formula below whenever you're choosing a pair. Incorporate the following guide to your preferred trading strategy so that you won't lose any money.

Remember that choosing the right pair can help you increase returns, but if you choose the wrong one, you will lose money.

Firstly, identify the trends. This is the first step you should take whenever you're looking for a currency pair to trade.

A trend represents historical data points and the direction wherein the Forex market has moved in the past.

For example, the exchange rate of the JPY/USD pair has been decreasing in the past six months. By applying MAs or using trend lines to your charts, you can identify trends. You should also take note of sideway trends. If the movement of the price is in a horizontal direction, then the price is stable and the forces of demand or supply are almost equal.

In case you don't know, a trend is the tendency of a price to move in a particular direction within a specific period. A trend can be downward, sideways, upward, short-term, or long-term.

Successful and profitable Forex transactions that come with a high return are associated with the trader's ability to identify trends. They use the data they've collected to choose the best position for their trades. They know when is the best time to open or close a position.

Second, pair your preferred trading strategy with your chosen trends. The currency pair that you should choose must be a trending pair so that you can apply your trading strategy in your decisions. Does it fluctuate too much?

If so, then purchase it at one of its lowest points and sell it at its highest point.

It's important to consider sideway trends as stated above.

But, if you choose a pair that only moves horizontally, it will be hard for you to gain profit or foresee future price movements. If you still intend to do this, look at other indicators, such as economic and political factors.

Third, take note of the ATR or the Average True Range of a currency pair. This is the average movement in pips in just one day.

What's the significance of ATR in trading?

When choosing the currency pair for your trades, the ATR can help.

If you want to limit your losses, you will either trade with a stop-loss order or limit your investment.

For the former, the ATR is integral, especially if you can't determine the moving average of a particular currency pair.

The ATR is an indicator used for technical analysis. It measures market volatility by decomposing the entire range of a currency's price for a given period. It can show how much a pair moves on average.

This indicator can help you specify the best time for placing a stop-loss order and opening a position.

In addition to all of that, the ATR of the pair you're eyeing can ascertain whether or not it's compatible with your trading objective and strategy. If you trade aggressively, take note of the pairs with a high ATR since they fluctuate a lot.

Knowing the ATR of your preferred pair brings a huge difference in the failure or success of your trades.

Chapter 11

Frequently Asked Questions

Although Forex is the biggest financial market in the whole world, it's an unfamiliar terrain to many people. Those who have no prior experience in currency trading may find the endeavor tricky and complicated. Until the emergence of online trading, when the accesses to FX markets were limited, hedge funds, multinational corporations, and financial institutions dominated foreign exchanges.

Now, times have changed. Information about currency trading is all around social media. Advertisements for trading platforms entice young and old alike. Retail and individual traders crave for information. They want to know more about how one can earn profits at home without having to go outside. Most small businesses require several thousands of dollars to earn at least fifteen to twenty percent return.

In truth, trading currencies can be relatively easy, especially if you have an idea about exchange rates. However, the planning part and the methods and indicators used to predict trends and price action can be daunting upon the first encounter.

With Forex and with efficient trading strategies, you can acquire at least thirty percent of your principal every month. With everything you've learned so far, you won't say that that is too good to be true.

Before you end your journey, don't forget the FAQs, or the cheat sheet for currency trading.

Frequently Asked Questions

- How does the foreign exchange market compare to other financial markets?

Unlike futures, options, or stocks, Forex trading doesn't transpire on a regulated exchange. No governing body directly controls foreign exchange markets. Participants trade based on credit agreements.

- What are the major currencies?

Some retail dealers buy and sell exotic currencies, like the Czech koruna or Thai baht. Most dealers, however, trade using the seven major pairs in the world.

- USD/CHF
- GBP/USD
- USD/JPY
- EUR/USD
- NZD/USD
- USD/CAD
- AUD/USD

The pairs above, along with the EUR/GBP, GBP/JPY, and EUR/JPY, make up over ninety-five percent of all the speculative trades in Foreign exchange markets worldwide.

• What's a carry trade in Forex?

Carry is the most prominent type of transaction in the Forex market. Retail speculators and hedge funds often prefer a currency carry trade over other types of Forex transactions. In a carry trade, an investor borrows a currency at a low-interest rate in order to purchase another currency. In other words, the trader targets a

currency with a high-interest rate, and he will then buy a specific amount using another currency with a low-interest rate.

• What's a Forex commission?

Traders who buy and sell options, futures, or currencies need a broker acting as an agent. The broker delivers the order to a Forex market and executes it based on the trader's instructions. For providing his service, the agent is given a commission when the investor has traded the financial instrument.

• In currency trading, what is margin?

Margin is the amount of money required in your broker account in order to secure a particular open position. The amount depends on the broker and the transaction agreements.

- How can I begin trading currencies?

First, you must register an account with a Forex broker like AGEA and eToro. After this, you use the broker's client program to trade currencies. The process usually takes less than ten minutes.

- Who owns the foreign exchanges?

Foreign exchanges are interbank markets. No one owns any of the FX markets around the world. This implies that each Forex deal is conducted between two participants only. They're the seller and the buyer. Forex isn't connected to any government, country, or organization.

- What are the work hours of the Forex market?

The FX market is available from GMT 22:00 Sunday to GMT 22:00 Friday.

- What are short and long positions?

Any sell position is a short position. This means that it will be profitable if the exchange rate increases.

Any buy position is a long position. This implies that the position will be profitable if the exchange rate decreases.

- What's the best strategy for currency trading?

In truth, there's none. Every market condition should be dealt with a particular trading strategy. Particular currency trading strategies can only be effective for specific pairs and for a limited time.

- How much money does an individual need to start trading in the market?

Some FX brokers allow for trading for as little as 1 USD. The minimum amount depends on the broker or brokerage platform.

- Can I trade Forex if I don't want to install a trading platform?

If you don't want to use a platform, then go for website-based foreign exchanges. Here are some examples:

- Oanda

- Exnes

- RoboForex

- Interactive Brokers

- Can I open a long position in EUR/USD pair and withdraw in euros?

The answer is "No." You possibly can't. In spot Forex, there's no delivery.

- What's a spread in FX trading?

Brokers quote two different prices for each pair: the bid and ask price. The "bid" is the selling price of the first currency. The "ask" is the buying price of the first currency in a pair. The difference between the "bid" and "ask" price is the "spread." This is also known as the "bid/ask spread."

Brokers who don't ask for commissions earn with the bid/ask spread. The fee for their service(s) is included in the buy and sell price of the pair being traded. They earn a profit by selling a domestic currency for a higher price than what they have paid. They also make money when they buy a currency from you.

- Why do all of my open trades start in a loss?

When opening a transaction in a foreign exchange, you either do it at "Bid price for Sell trades" or "at the Ask price for Buy trades." The same rule is applicable in calculating the transaction's floating loss or profit.

Therefore, a newly opened trade always starts in the red because of the Bid/Ask spread.

This is the reason why traders should beat the Bid/Ask spread first so that their investment would become profitable.

- How can I compete with large financial organizations?

When trading, banks employ seasoned professionals who use fundamental analysis before engaging in a transaction. They often look at the unemployment rate, GDP, and inflation in the two countries whose domestic currencies are involved in the exchange.

Such traders utilize both technical and fundamental analysis when looking at indicators and predicting price action.

They read charts and graphs to interpret the market sentiment and crowd psychology surrounding a particular pair.

For example, if you want to take a buy position on EUR/USD, you should look at technical indicators associated with the pair. In doing so, you can evaluate its market history.

Henceforth, you must do the same things that the people with training and experience do. Look at Forex news, prices, studies, and opinions.

Most platforms provide charts and other visuals that offer information about the latest market trends, as well as URLs to third- party websites. These are usually found in the commentary section.

Conclusion

At this point, you probably already know the dos and don'ts in Forex trading. Now, you can start trading currencies safely. To sum up everything you've learned, here's a short step-by-step synopsis.

First, you have to create an account on a licensed and regulated brokerage platform. Make sure that you have a good internet connection if you want to trade Forex. You'll need it when you're looking at trends and relevant economic data.

Second, read forex quotes and choose a currency pair.

Third, know the indicators that you can use to study the exchange rate and your preferred pair. Once you've listed your indicators, choose a trading strategy for your style and account size.

Fourth, study the price action and the price movement of the currency pair. Research additional data like market sentiment and economic events that have affected past exchange rates.

Fifth, analyze the market. Consider the risks and look at the factors that could affect future prices.

Sixth, plot the points and chart indexes. With the data you've gathered, predict the different price movements that could occur in the future. Lastly, calculate the profits from your predicted situations.

Seventh, determine the margin of your trade.

Depending on the policies of your broker, you may just invest a small amount of money, but make sure that you can still earn a high profit. If you can predict future exchange rates accurately, your trading decisions will be successful. You'll experience winning streaks instead of losing streaks.

Eight, place your order.

Lastly, watch your losses and profits and study the results of each of your trades. Learn from your mistakes and don't forget to watch the trends and patterns.

Do have fun trading currencies! But, don't forget to be vigilant and be wise at all times.

I'd like to thank you and congratulate you for transiting my lines from start to finish.

I hope this book was able to help you to win big in the Forex market.

The next step is to choose a broker and create a trading account, so you can start trading soonest.

I wish you the best of luck!

www.ingramcontent.com/pod-product-compliance
Lightning Source LLC
Chambersburg PA
CBHW071644210326
41597CB00017B/2106